CW00482302

Becoming

A Very Long Walk &
The Awakening of a Woman

by India L Hicks

India Lauren Hicks lives in Cornwall by the sea with her gorgeous partner Kev. She can be found sewing beautiful garments for her business, ILH Handcrafted, and selling them at Artisan markets, tending to her vegetable garden and returning back to her beloved coast path time and time again.

Instagram: @ilhhandcrafted
Website: www.ilhhandcrafted.com

Self-published via Kindle Direct Publishing.
First published 15th June 2022.
Second edition published February 2024.
Copyright © India Hicks 2022. All rights reserved.
ISBN: 9798875668913
For anonymity reasons, some names in this book have been changed.

No part of this book may be reproduced in any form or by any means without written permission from the author except for the use of brief quotations in a book review.

Cover & map design: Kev Chan @kevthepainter

India L Hicks

Portrait by Drew Graves @drew_graves99

Chapters

Opening

This is the story of one woman's journey back to herself. On a 630 mile long path beside the ocean. Where crashing waves meet sweeping skies. Salt, sun, sand, surf, wind, rain. Where all the elements combine into Mother Nature's most glorious orchestral symphony.

India found herself on this very path, The South West Coast Path in Britain, alone, with nothing but a backpack full of food and water and a little green circular pop-up tent to keep her alive.

After escaping a life of emotional turmoil in an unhealthy relationship, she was about to embark on an epic adventure of love, loss and awakening.

"To anyone who is standing on a precipice in their life. To anyone who is sitting on the fence of making a life-changing decision. To my fellow women past, present and future. I hope my story inspires you. To save your life as I have saved mine. Because no one else has the power to do it for you, only you hold that special magic within yourself.

My advice to you, if you will have me, is to just go for it. If every fibre of your being wants you to do this thing that you've been dreaming of for years, then do it. You won't know how, you won't know what the path ahead will bring, but you will be safe in the knowledge that you are following what is good and true for you. And that is all we can ever do in this precious life of ours.

And in this book I will share with you, dear reader, my precipice, my beloved path, my very long, winding, beloved path to becoming, and coming home to, myself." - India L Hicks

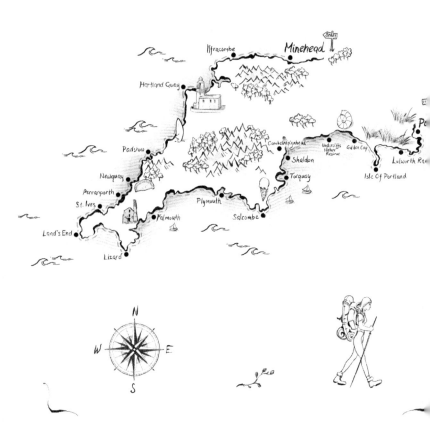

Prologue

Saturday, January 2nd, 2021.

"Oh god, I'm sorry, I'm so sorry, everything's such a mess!" I sobbed down the phone to his sister-in-law.

"India, I don't understand... why?? You two seemed so happy! I don't understand?!" she replied confused after I'd told her what just happened..

"It's... such a... mess... no one knew anything... he didn't want me to say anything..." I rasped through the tears as my mum sped us down the dual carriageway away from my old life, a hastily packed bag of clothes and toiletries shoved onto the backseat of her car.

"I had to leave him, there's so much you don't know. Just please, please go sit with him. Please, he can't be alone, I'm so terrified of what he might do, please don't let him be alone!" I rambled frantically, my mind whizzing with the ramifications of what I'd just done.

"I can't believe this is happening. OK, I'm five mins away from your place. I'll go there right now. India, I don't know what's happened, but please give me a call when things have calmed down, OK?" With that, she hung up.

My Mum gazed at me with tears in her eyes as she tried to focus on the road.

"Oh my baby..." was all she could say.

We finally pulled up outside my best friend's house. My safe haven, where we'd planned my escape. Betsy flung open her front door as I ran into her arms.
"Shh, shh, you're here now. It's over, you're safe, I'm here, it's ok, you're safe now." she whispered into my ear, stroking my hair as I sobbed into her shoulder.

Week 1 – Out of My Depth

Five months later, and I was on my way towards the biggest adventure of my life. For the previous eight years I'd been trapped inside a deeply unhappy, unhealthy relationship. I had escaped in January, been through a rollercoaster of emotions, self-discoveries, intense inner work and now I was about to embark on a journey that would really test what I was made of.

The month after I'd left my ex, who shall remain anonymous in this book, is a bit of a blur now. A blur of sleepless nights, tears and numbness. For the first week, I lived at Betsy's place for which I am eternally grateful to her. She is more than my best friend, she is my soul-sister and I'm so thankful to have someone like her in my life. She helped me pick myself up off the floor and put the fragments of myself back together again. We cooked nourishing meals together, watched trashy period dramas on tv and drank endless cups of soothing rooibos tea. After that, I moved in with my Dad, Step-Mum and brothers and started to try and heal myself. To put back together the shattered pieces of my heart and soul.

One night in late January a few days after I'd moved into my Dad's place, I couldn't stop crying. I'd been crying myself to sleep for the past few nights just feeling lost, wondering where my life was going, not sure of who I was. I'd been feeling a strong sense of guilt, failure and frustration that I couldn't save my relationship. That I couldn't save *him*. Couldn't I have tried a little bit harder? Given a little bit more of myself away? Is he ok? Is he going to kill himself?

It was a little after midnight and I went outside to the garden, wrapped up in my duvet, and sat on the patio looking up at the clear sky and the abundance of stars. There was a biting chill in the air that stung my cheeks and made my nose run. I was beginning to feel again. A galaxy full of twinkling dots shined down on me. Clusters and swirls here and there, and larger spotlights proudly suspended against the black space around them. They looked so beautiful, I sobbed at the sight of them. Sobbed through my pain. I asked them, "Please help me, I don't know what to do. Please, please, please…" And in that very moment, the most beautiful shooting star swiftly but gently arced its way across the entire sky.

"Walk, India."

A whisper. An instruction from somewhere, or someone, deep within me, around me, above me. It didn't sound like a particularly male or a particularly female voice, but for some reason I felt like I had known them. Or it. Or whoever it was. I'd had a complicated relationship with God and religion growing up. But in that moment, I suddenly felt a sense of calm wash over me, everything was going to be ok. A higher energy, whatever that may be, was showing me the way. I will heal myself, I thought. I will go away somewhere, anywhere, on my own, follow my intuition and work through my issues.

A couple of months later, Mum and I moved into a lovely little flat deep in the countryside by the sea together. She'd been living in a motor home for the past two years by this point, so I'm so grateful to her for helping me out both emotionally and financially in that way. I didn't know what the future held, but one thing was for sure - I was relieved. Relieved that I no longer had to endure the emotional abuse. I could start afresh and achieve everything I dreamed of in life. I settled into life by the ocean. My cocoon era. Going for daily power-walks amongst the pebbles and seaweed. Allowing my mind to roam as well as my feet.

Since I saw the shooting star that night a few weeks previously, something had been nudging at my heart. A yearning, a restlessness, an idea I'd had as a teenager long ago but never dreamed would be a possibility, but now pressed against my soul like an urgent siren call: to walk all 630 miles of the South West Coast Path, all in one go, all on my own. It would take six weeks, walking 15 miles a day with me carrying all the things I needed to survive on my back and wild camping along the way. I had to do it. It was just the thing I needed - to do something for myself, to have an adventure and heal properly on my own.

I'd walked small local day-trip sections of the SWCP countless times before, some sections were as familiar as the back of my hand, and yet to walk all of it in one go was something I knew I just had to do. I started to put together plans to make it a reality and set the date.

In the month leading up to my walk I started doing my best to prepare, doing fitness training, gathering my equipment and researching the route. Although, I would soon find out that no amount of training could have prepared me for what was to come. I got my old friend, my Osprey backpack that I trekked with across Mexico, Belize & the Caribbean one summer 11 years ago, out of storage that had been gathering dust for the past eight years.

Doing my first test run with her on my back, I got unexpectedly emotional. We'd had such amazing adventures together in my late teens but during my twenties I had lost my way and she'd sat neglected, pining to be used again. But slipping her onto my back for that first test walk, feeling the cushioned sturdiness of her straps, the resilient fabric, the way she takes care in evenly distributing the weight of the contents inside, still as strong and as beautiful quality as the day I bought her, I felt that same wanderlust come rushing back as I had felt at 17, it felt like coming home. My eyes couldn't help but fill with tears, it felt so amazing to be reunited with her again, finally coming back to my authentic, curious, adventurous self.

I scoured various hiking blogs and articles on what I'd need for a long distance trip and wrote out the following equipment list:

Camping Gear
- Backpack & waterproof inner bag
- Tent & rubber mallet
- Sleeping bag, blow-up pillow & sleeping mat
- Camping stove set & spare gas

Clothing
- 2x leggings, 1x shorts, 3x t-shirts, 3x knickers, 3x socks, 1x bra
- 1x fleece, 1x waterproof jacket, 1x waterproof trousers
- 1x pair of walking shoes, 1x pair of walking sandals
- 1x sunhat, 1x swimsuit, 1x pair of sunglasses

Toiletries
- Microfibre towel
- Deodorant, wet-wipes & soap

- Toothpaste & toothbrush
- Sunscreen, lip-balm & moisturiser
- Comb & hair-bands
- Loo roll & sanitary pads

Food
- 10l waterbag & electrolyte tablets
- 30x military food ration packs
- Protein bars & protein shake powder
- Porridge oats
- Kendall mint cake
- Tea
- Nuts & seeds mix

Miscellaneous
- Walking poles
- Camping lamp, matches & lighter
- First aid kit including ***BLISTER PLASTERS***
- Whistle, multi-tool knife & self defence spray
- Water bottle & water purifier tablets
- SWCP guidebook & maps
- Plastic trowel & small binbags
- Phone, solar battery pack, spare battery pack, headphones
- Tick remover
- Book, journal, pen
- Bumbag & day bag

The weekend before my big walk quickly rolled around. I'd handed my resignation letter in to my day job eight weeks previously, I had been assistant manager at the indie boutique, Fifty5a, full time for the past nine years, and it was an emotional goodbye to all my lovely customers, colleagues and amazing bosses Malin & Aron who I was so so grateful to for the steady, supportive years of employment. I had all my equipment, I was feeling strong and ready. Now all I had to do was do the actual thing. I'd be lying if I said I wasn't bloody rattling with nerves. But I was nervous in a good way - it was my soul's purpose to do this walk. I felt it to my core.

Monday the 31st of May 2021. Time to do it.

Dad drove me up to Minehead, the start point, with my step-mum and my brothers in the car as well. All the way up it still didn't feel real that I was actually about to embark on this journey. When we finally got there, I said my goodbyes to my lovely family in front of the giant grey steel monument depicting two hands holding a map that marks the start of the epic 630 mile trail. My 30cm-wide home for the foreseeable future. I really fought to hold back the tears. I didn't want them to see me cry, I wanted to reassure them that I've got this, I can do this, I'm strong enough.

My Dad is my hero. He's so fiercely protective like a lioness with her cub, unashamedly emotional, infinitely loving and is the best role model for what a man should be, but I will always be his little girl in his eyes and I could tell that me going on this trip was causing a lot of anxiety for him, especially after everything I'd been through. So I only let myself cry after I'd taken those first few steps away from them and into the wilderness. Where my soul was meant to be.

With tears in my eyes, butterflies in my stomach and a steely determination in my heart I took my first steps on the path. It felt so surreal, I couldn't believe I was actually doing it. I felt like a newborn deer, just learning how to walk; my legs were all jellied, my feet didn't really feel attached to my body, my arms felt awkward and unnatural holding the walking poles, my pack...

Ohhh my dear backpack felt so incredibly heavy. I couldn't put it on while standing up, my arms weren't strong enough yet to lift it, so I had to perform a ridiculous looking routine of sitting down, strapping myself in, rocking forwards onto my hands and knees and then using my poles to lift myself up. It was probably around 30kg, which is well over half my body weight of 54kg.

The tent I'd bought for the trip was a little khaki green pop up tent that folded up into a coordinating circular bag. It was too wide to fit into my pack so I had to strap it to the outside with bungee cords and it made me look like a Teenage Mutant Ninja Turtle. I was grateful for my poles adding some stability because my balance was totally out of whack carrying such a wide heavy load.

The path starting from Minehead was rather hilly. No, that's an understatement: it was almost mountainous. It went through beautiful old woodlands hugging the cliff face and even though my shoulders and hips were already becoming sore from the weight of my pack, I was just totally buzzing to be starting this adventure. I am alone, but I could never be lonely as long as I follow my true soul path, I thought.

Climbing through one section of woodland a couple hours in, I passed a woman in her 40s on a run.

"That's a lot of stuff you've got there." she said with a look of concern on her face.

"Hi! Yes I'm hiking the entire South West Coast Path in one go. This is my first day. I'm quite nervous!" I replied, red faced, sweaty and out of breath from the steep incline.

"Oh good for you! I've done it all too. Ran it in 40 days for my 40th birthday. Didn't carry as much as you though. Had a support team with me. Are you sure you need all of that?" Running woman said.

"Wow that's amazing, I think it's going to take me a lot longer than 40 days to do this... and I can already think of some things I can get rid of..." I said, trailing off with a slight flush of embarrassment. Gosh, she must think I'm totally naive and inexperienced, I thought... and she'd be right if she was thinking that.

"Well go steady, stay safe and look after yourself ok?" and with that, off she went like a graceful gazelle through the woods. And off I went, a slow, naive, out of breath Turtle.

Two cliff climbs later.

"Fuuuuuuuuck, why did I decide to do this?!"
"Urrrrrrrrrgggggghhhhh..."
"Aaaaaaaaoooooooohhhhhh... OK. Get to that tree right there. And then have a little rest."
I got to my rest-tree, four hours into my walk, only six miles in on my first day and I was absolutely exhausted. I was coming to the very swift realisation that I probably wouldn't be able to do 15 miles a day yet. And it was probably going to take me more than six weeks to do this.
"OK. Now get to that fern bush. Then have another little rest."
"OK. Now get to that rock. Then have another little rest."
"Come on India. You... can... do... this."
"You can fucking do this. You can fucking do this."
"Oh my gosh... can I do this?"

A couple hours later I finally almost made it to Porlock Weir where I'd planned to stop for the day. There was just a mile of pebble beach to cross to get there. I had a sudden rush of energy at the thought that I'd almost completed my first day and so I set off along the pebble beach. There was a sign a little way along that said

"WARNING. Porlock Weir inaccessible due to river breach. Do not proceed any further." Pfffft, I thought. I can't see a river breach?! How bad could it be? Porlock Weir is right there a ¼ mile in the distance, let's carry on and if I need to paddle across a little stream, well, that might be quite refreshing.

Shit... Shit. Shit. Shit on it!!!!

I got to the breach. It was a deep, smelly bog running from the wet marshland on my left, through the pebble beach and into the dark sea on my right. There were flies buzzing around everywhere feasting on the salty sweat beading from my skin and I was completely wiped out from walking on the tricky pebble terrain whilst carrying almost 30kg of weight on my back. I had a total meltdown. I cried at my own stupidity.
"Rookie mistake, India!! How could you be so stupid?! Always. Pay. Attention. To. The. Signs!!! Oh no, oh no, oh no. I'm gunna have to turn around and go all the way back to the start of the beach and take the inland path!" I wailed. This is not a good start.

So back I plodded along the beach to the official inland path. My shoulders, lower back and hips were raw and bruised, crying out to take the bloody pack off. I reached the inland path and started to walk the correct final mile to my finish point. I got to half a mile away, but couldn't go any further, my legs were done, my back was done, I was done.

I set up wild-camp on a little grassy patch beside the path that overlooked the lush green marsh, the pebble beach beyond and the ocean beyond that and crawled into my tent. The sun was just beginning to set over the water and the sky turned gentle shades of pink, orange and red. It was beautiful. And for the hundredth time that day, I cried. Big, fat, salty tears spilled down my face as the enormity of what I was doing suddenly hit me. Life changes so quickly. In the space of a few months I'd gone through such a lot. And now I was here. Fulfilling my dreams. It felt so surreal, feeling all these mixed emotions. Pain at the traumas of the past few years, relief that I was finally free from it, and pride that I was grabbing life by the balls and bloody well having a good go at it.

Ping! A text on my phone. A lifeline of support. Betsy. She'd sent me a voice note full of loving words of encouragement to check in with me to see if I was ok. I cried more as I listened to her voice note on repeat about 50 times. Soaking up her soothing words like moisturiser on my cracked nerves. I sent her an emotional one back, telling her not to worry, I'm fine, I'm fine, I'm fine.

I devoured my first camp meal of vegetarian bean stew, too impatient to wait for it to fully heat up on my tiny camping stove. These military ration packs don't look the most appealing, but my gosh, it tasted so damn good. I snuggled up in my sleeping bag and tried my best to calm my nerves at the fact I was wild-camping. Alone. The sun set and the sounds of the night-time nature came alive. My senses heightened as birds sang their evensong in the trees behind me, the waves gently rumbled in the distance and various rustling sounds came from the marsh in front of the path. Every noise amplified to a deafening volume as my skin prickled with self-awareness.

I willed myself for sleep to come and take me, but it never did. Every sound coming from outside my tent made me jump. I was clutching my self defence spray so tightly to my chest in case some kidnapper came and kidnapped me. Or in case a bear came and mauled me in the night. Of course, there are no wild bears in the UK but my overactive imagination was thinking up all these scenarios and freaking myself out. I couldn't get in a comfy position either, the hardness of the ground made my hips and knees ache as if I was 68, not 28. I kept listening to Betsy's voice note like it was a comfort blanket.

Eventually the all encompassing darkness of night started to lighten, the warm yellow tones of sunrise waking the birds up for their morning chorus. And I was still awake, but feeling a lot more jaded now. My eyes felt as dry and shrivelled as raisins, my legs as stiff as wood and my back was even more sore than the previous day. But I dragged myself out of my sleeping bag anyway, nature was indeed calling and I needed to find somewhere to relieve the urgent pressure in my bowels immediately. I must say, wild-pooing certainly is an experience... of course I dug a hole and left no trace as any good human should do, but it sure makes one appreciate the modern luxury of an actual toilet.

Day two. Ok this is getting really fucking hard now. More yo-yo-ing up and down small mountains, more soreness in my back and now I'm pretty sure I can feel some blisters forming on the pads of my feet. It was very slow progress and I had to stop to rest a lot. I was pushing it if I was doing more than one mile an hour. But the VIEWS. Oh my... the views made it so worth it. The ocean was sparkling blue, the black cliffs of the northern side of the SWCP dramatic, breathtaking and humbling in their size. I passed through more woodland hugging the cliff faces, some beautiful waterfalls and rugged headland bursting with wildflowers of the brightest blue, red and yellow.

I finally got to Lynmouth, 13 miles later, absolutely on the brink of collapse. I staggered around the small village for a while trying to find a suitable place to wild-camp, but I'd been walking since 8am, it was nearing 7:30pm and I couldn't find anywhere. I stumbled into the Captain's House B&B and when the lovely elderly gentleman who owned it welcomed me in and said he had a room available, I burst into tears of relief.

Poor chap, he probably felt overwhelmed at the sight of this sweaty, smelly, bedraggled young woman collapsing into tears in his hallway. He must've taken pity on me as he instantly fixed me up a cream tea for supper in the garden after he showed me to my room. His kindness just made me cry more.

Now, I don't like cream tea, (I know what you're thinking, "what?! Someone from the Westcountry not liking cream tea?!") scones and cream are just not my thing. But this. Oh, this was the best thing I've ever tasted. Warm fluffy scones with a crisp outer crust, silky sweet raspberry jam and thick soft cream washed down with the best cup of tea I've ever had. I closed my eyes and lifted my face to the sky with a sigh of rapturous bliss. Heaven.

Afterwards, I went upstairs to my room and began to really soak in my surroundings for the evening. It really is a gorgeous little B&B with chintz everywhere you look. From the rose and lilac floral bedding with matching curtains to the salmon pink wash basin, mahogany furniture and old fashioned persian-style carpets. Very Fawlty Towers, but with a much nicer host.

I went across the hallway to the shared bathroom, more pastel coloured porcelain, and had the most amazing shower. I felt the warm water wash away the salt from my sweat and tears, soothe the friction burns on my back and shoulders and relax the tired muscles in my legs. It was only my second day, but it felt like I'd been hiking for an eternity. I was really proud of the distance covered though. 13 miles total!

Bed. So soft. So warm. So comforting. I fell asleep quickly. The gentle sound of the river outside the B&B soothing me to a deep sleep like the lullabies Mum sang to me as a child.

I woke up incredibly stiff and sore despite my best efforts to massage and stretch my legs out before bed last night. Hobbling down the stairs and into the breakfast room, I met the other guests staying here, a couple in their 60s and a young family with two kids, and they were all very interested to know what I was doing. The father of the young family warned me that there were more tough sections coming up and my heart sank a little. According to my SWCP Association guide book it was meant to be getting easier after today... hmm, I guess time will tell who is right.

The breakfast at the Captain's House B&B was amazing and hearty and I think I polished it off in two minutes flat. Sausages, bacon, beans, mushrooms, tomato, buttery toast, the proper thing. I'd been following a vegan and gluten-free diet since January simply because it made my body feel amazing. But I realised quickly on this walk that I can't afford to be picky about what I eat. I'm going to need all the energy, calories and protein I can get if I don't want my muscles wasting away.

I went back up to my room after breakfast and started to pack my things away, feeling more than a little bit of dread at the thought of another day of being in pain. I strapped the pads of my feet up with blister plasters and surgical tape to protect the now very tender pieces of flesh between my big toes and middle toes and slowly lifted my pack onto my sore back, wincing as the pressure loaded onto my small frame. "Right," I said shakily out loud, giving myself a little pep talk and blinking back tears of pain, "just take it slow today. Don't pressure yourself to do the miles. Just take it slow and try to enjoy it. That's what you came here to do. ENJOY it."

Day three's route climbed incredibly steeply out of Lynmouth and through the stunning Valley of the Rocks area. The weather was overcast and warm with a cool breeze - perfect for hiking. I tried my hardest to appreciate it, really I did. The Valley of the Rocks is one of the SWCP highlights, but I was in so much pain. My legs were screaming for mercy, my shoulder blades were starting to develop swollen bumps, my lower back had sore, weeping friction burns, and my stomach was constantly grumbling for all the carbs. I was still only managing one mile an hour.

"Ok ok ok... get to that rock there..."

"Fucking do it India. Get to that grassy patch now."

"You can fucking do it. You can fucking do it. Now get to that flower."

"You have no choice. You have to do it. You can fucking do it."

On and on this rather harsh motivational solo conversation continued (throughout most of the first two weeks in fact). It seemed to really work though, giving myself little goals like getting to a particular rock or flower or fern gave me little boosts of achievement and really helped to push me through. Another thing that really helped was singing to myself. A repetitive internal playlist of "Send Me on My Way" by Rusted Root, "Les Fleurs" by Minnie Ripperton and "A Head Full of Dreams" by Coldplay helped a little bit to distract myself from the pain my body was in. I didn't care that people passing by must've thought I was crazy. I am a little unhinged, I think all the best people are.

I could only manage six and a half miles on that third day. Stumbling down into the Heddon River valley, voice rasping with the effort, almost in tears again, I found a lovely little wild-camping spot in the woods by the gently bubbling river

and collapsed with relief that I was done walking
for the day. Shortly after, a very beautiful looking
young family walked by, all clean and well
dressed and smelling nice. The son of about
seven or eight with long curly hair down to his
shoulders came up to me with a slightly
suspicious look in his big brown eyes.
"What are you doing?" he said with the
directness that comes with being that age.
"I'm hiking the South West Coast Path and I'm
stopping here to wild-camp for the evening.'' I
replied, trying my best to seem non-threatening,
cheerful even and not the grumpy, tired, crazy
person I felt.
"Oh. That's cool. Why don't you stay in a hote-"
"-Sorry about him, he's so curious all the time! He
loves camping. Come on, love, don't disturb the
lady." said a woman butting in who must've
been his mum, a beautiful woman with long
brown hair down to her waist. I couldn't tell if she
was concerned about him "disturbing" me or
really me disturbing him...
"Oh I don't mind at all!... I'm camping because I
can't afford to stay in hotels all the time... but it's
amazing to get out in nature like this isn't it?"
trying even harder to seem friendly now.
"That's really cool, I'd love to do what you're
doing one day." he said, his big eyes had that
spark of wanderlust I knew so well.
"Well it was lovely to meet you, good luck with
your journey!" the mum said, ushering him away.
I really hoped he would fuel that spark of
wanderlust. Society is so quick to squash that

sense of adventure out of kids, I wish all people could retain their curiosity and their childlike wanderlust.

It was bliss to crawl into my tent in my sleeping bag and listen to the birds in the trees, the river gently rolling by. It was a little chilly in that valley so I prepared dinner rations wrapped up in my sleeping bag. Vegetarian curry and rice heated through on my tiny camping stove and a granola bar. Tasty but no way near enough sustenance. I was still ravenous, but sleep was starting to take me so I quickly brushed my teeth, wiped myself down with a wet wipe and snuggled in for the night.

Day four. I woke up with the sunrise and tried to sit up. But wait. Why can't I move?, I wondered. My body had seized hard overnight. "UGGGGGHHHHHHH!!!" I wiggled my toes, tears already in my eyes at the pain my body was waking up to. Gently, gently, gently I started to make small movements, rolling my shoulders, flexing my knee joints, rolling my ankles around. This must be what elderly people feel like, I thought. I'd never felt so grateful to be able bodied in my life. I realised how precious our bodies are, how much we need to treasure them and look after them.

I did my best to massage my legs and get the muscles warmed up for the day, trying to get some of that crystallised lactic acid flushing through. After my breakfast blend of porridge, protein powder, nuts and seeds, I did some gentle yoga which did help a little.

"Ok, India. We've got a big one today. Great Hangman. You can do it. Just take it slow." giving myself another pep talk. Great Hangman is an iconic part of the North Devon coast. A small mountain climbing up at 1014 feet, it would either make or break me, but I was excited and determined to find out.

Climbing through the woods out of the Heddon River valley, I actually felt ok. "Maybe... I'm... Getting... Stronger!" I said excitedly between breaths as I got to the top, gasping for more oxygen but feeling exhilarated. It was rather windy as I kept my eyes firmly fixed to the lichen adorned path that hugged the rocky cliff tops. My pack still felt so heavy, my tent an annoyingly wide load on this narrow path, in these strong winds. Anxiety crept into my gut as I imagined myself flying off the cliff into the depths below. "You'll be fine, India. Go steady. Gooooooo steady now." I couldn't let these thoughts consume me. I had to stay focussed.

The path to Great Hangman didn't actually feel too tiring. It was so beautiful, on one headland I really got into my stride, skipping over the confetti of sheep poo that dotted this section of the path, the brisk wind whipping my hair into a tangled mess resembling spun sugar, my heart filling with hope that it was finally getting a little easier. I could finally appreciate some of the majesty that surrounded me: the sea was a dramatic shade of navy accented with bright white curls of crashing waves, the black cliffs humbled me with their proud, jagged silhouettes, and the smell of the fresh air cleansed my lungs, I couldn't help myself but howl like a wolf sometimes. It was the only noise that expressed how I felt, words just didn't seem enough. This path. This journey. I'm meant to be here.

Well, shit.

I'd paused by the bubbling stream at the bottom of the valley before Great Hangman. I hastily had a wee in a bush and ate a granola bar and some Kendall Mint Cake to prepare me for what was to come. I looked up. "Ohhhhh my... that's a long way up." I said to myself, pointing out the bleeding obvious. Well, nothing else for it but to climb. And so, I did. One foot in front of the other, back bent forward 45 degrees, my arms holding my walking poles helping to thrust me forward, my pack squeaking as well as I with the effort, the backs of my legs screaming again for a ceasefire. I stop often, carrying on with my motivational speeches of "Get to that bush there!" and "You. Can. Fucking. Do. It!" - I may get those carved on my tombstone, I think to myself.

I have many more emotional breakdowns before I reach the summit, what's new? But when I do reach the summit, oh my, once again I yo-yo between emotions of exasperation and complete joy at what I feel so grateful to witness. Panoramic views as far as the eye can see of the rugged coastline, Exmoor, the Devon countryside and little towns and villages dotted about here and there amongst the lush green land.

I begin the descent into the small town of Combe Martin, it's long, sometimes steep and sometimes slippery with the dusty gravel terrain and brings a fresh hell of pain to the front of my thighs. I'm half a mile away from Newberry Campsite where I'd planned to stop for the day but I can't take one more step. The path has come out onto a winding country road and yet again I'm close to tears with pain, every cell in my body hurts, I felt like I could collapse at any moment. So I do something I've never done before that in normal circumstances would terrify me, but not today. Today I'm desperate. I stick my thumb out and try to hitch a lift.

As soon as I do, an angel appears in the form of a middle aged lady with her young daughter winding down the road in her old, dented silver hatchback. It's full to the brim with stuff in boxes and I'm not sure if there's any space for me and my massive pack.
"Hi! I'm trying to get to Newberry campsite, I'm hiking the coast path but I'm so tired, I can't take another step" I explain.

"Oh you poor love, come on, hop in, you'll have to move a few bits out the way though, I'm afraid!" She says in a cheerful tone, adding, "We get loads of hikers round here, Newberry's a lovely place, you're not far away, but I can only imagine how you're feeling with that thing on your back!" "Oh thank you, thank you so much, I really appreciate it!" I reply, swallowing back the tears.

I do my best to "hop in" but it's a bit of a battle making space and then shoving my pack on top of the small mountain of stuff, trying carefully not to break anything that belongs to my knightess in shining (or not so shining as the case may be) armour. I make it in nonetheless and my body breathes a bittersweet sigh of relief at the feeling of a soft cushioned seat beneath me.

It's only a two minute drive down the valley and up a little bit to Newberry. My angel-hatchback-lady drops me off and says a cheerful goodbye and I hobble into the campsite reception where I'm greeted warmly by the young girl behind the counter. They are selling some basic food supplies and I get so overwhelmed and excited I dither a while at choosing some bits. I settled on a can of sparkling blood orange juice and a big bag of sour cream & chive flavoured lentil crisps.

Another lovely lady in her fifties, with cropped silver hair, large bosom and an aura about her

that just made me want to hug her, in a golf
buggy then takes me to my spot to camp in for
the night and she lends me a soft fluffy pink
towel after seeing my pathetic teatowel-sized
microfibre cloth I had planned to use.
"Good grief, my lovely, you can't use that thing to
dry yourself, you'll be there forever! Haha! The
shower and toilet block is just behind this hedge
here and we've even got a bath you can use."
Oh!!! A bath!!! Have I died and gone to heaven?

I flung up my tent, set up camp so quickly at the
prospect of a bath and hobbled over to the
shower block, my stiff body already starting to
relax at the sweet relief I was about to
experience… but… oh damn it. It's a paid-for one
that you have to insert coins in to get it to work…
"Urrrrggggggghhhhh" I groan… I stand there for
a couple minutes dithering at whether I can be
bothered to walk all the way back to reception to
get some change… "Oh I can't be bothered!
Shower it is!" I say outloud to myself. I stagger
into one of the showers which are really quite
luxurious with a little ledge that I just sit on with
the delicious hot water gushing over my sore
body. I massage myself under the water and I
think to myself that I could quite easily just sit
here forever.

Eventually I tear myself away from my steaming
hot sanctuary and head back to my tent for
dinner. I'm camped in a peaceful little quiet
section of the campsite with neatly maintained

grass and lush tall hedges surrounding me. On the menu tonight is veggie sausages in baked beans with the crisps and orange juice I bought earlier. I devour everything like a wild animal but it's not enough to satisfy my insatiable appetite. I'm sitting there feeling a bit sorry for myself when two glamorous blonde ladies in their fifties stroll by, each with a glass of prosecco in their hands. They must be sisters, I think to myself.

"Oh darlin', what yer doing all on your own there?"
"What's that dinner yer got there, that's not gunna fill y'up!" they both exclaim in their thick northern accents.
"Hi, I'm hiking the coast path and I'm carrying everything I need to survive so this is my rations that I'm eating" I replied feebly.
"Oh my goodness, right love yer not going to bed tonight without a hot cuppa tea in yer!"
"Exactly, right come on, come back to our motorhome, we'll give yer a nice cuppa tea, come on."
"Oh that's so kind of you, I would love that, thank you so much!" I reply, a small lump in my throat beginning to form, as they take my arms and usher me to their caravan..

I follow my new friends, Judith & Becky they're called, back to their fabulously luxurious motorhome and they instantly fix me up some hot sweet tea and toast with lashings of raspberry jam. They excitedly fuss over me as I tell them my story of how I came to be here and they quickly start to feel like my camp-mothers. They are so lovely and don't take no for an answer when they offer me more tea and more toast, both my heart and my belly become full with love. I tell them all about the struggles and triumphs I've had so far and they squeal and gasp in awe and wonder and say things like "You crazy little thing!" and "Oh I couldn't do what you're doing!"

They tell me lots about themselves too - how they are just two best friends from Lancashire who always make the effort to go away on holiday together to get a break from husbands and children and responsibilities. They drink lots of prosecco and always have a jolly good time.

The evening starts to close in and my eyes droop heavily from the day's exertion and full belly. I say my goodbyes to Judith & Becky and stagger back to my tent, feeling almost drunk from being so full. As I get back to my tent, I see that I have new neighbours - a group of three lads around my age are just setting up their tents. We exchange brief hellos, but I'm too tired at that point to delve into any deeper conversation. I hear Judith coming up behind me, "India love, here y'are, here's 'ot chocolate and some biccies to send yer off t'sleep, now y'can't go t'bed cold." she says, giving me a mug of sweet deliciousness and a tray of chocolate chip cookies.

"Oh, Judith, that's so wonderful, thank you so much!" I say with tears in my eyes, I feel so grateful to have met my camp-mothers, my heart feels so full at the human kindness I've experienced and I fall asleep quickly with happy thoughts of the adventures that tomorrow will bring.

Day five and I wake up early with the sunrise, my body starting to get used to being in its circadian rhythm now. I wolf down my breakfast and pack up as my camp neighbours are waking up too. They are three tall, handsome guys from London called Alastair, George & Aaron and they are on a week-long SWCP hiking trip from Minehead to Woolacombe, today is their last day, they are telling me. Alastair has bright blue eyes, freckles, swept back auburn hair and a well groomed beard. George has an almost 1940s look about him with a hipster moustache and short-back-and-sides. Aaron is the tallest of the three, with blonde highlighted hair swept back with a plastic black headband. All three are very fit and in good shape. I feel a bit embarrassed at my dishevelled appearance, but quickly forgive my ego for just wanting to have approval from the opposite sex.

They ask what I'm doing and I tell them my story briefly to which they seem very impressed. I tell them how I'm procrastinating at putting my pack on, I'm still in so much pain. But nothing for it but to just put it on and do it! Feeling embarrassment again as I perform my ridiculous sit-down routine of putting my pack on as they watch, I set off as the boys are tucking into their breakfast and feel buoyed on by their kind words of encouragement. I can do this, I think to myself. I'm a frickin' bad-ass, a lone female traveller, carrying this massive pack, I am a strong woman warrior!

Fucking coast path. Fucking backpack. Fucking heat. FUUUUUUUUCK!! I thought today was going to be easier. No more steep hills. I was wrong. Very wrong. The sun was blisteringly hot today with no cloud cover and the path offering no shade either. Yes, yes, the scenery is of course wonderful but it's lost its novelty somewhat today. The 12 miles I accomplished passed by in a blur of anger, pain, blood, sweat and tears. Every step was like a knife to my exhausted body. The blisters on the pads of my feet were now floppy pieces of flesh that looked like they would just slide right off at any moment. In fact - oh, there they go.

"Why the hell did you decide to do this, India?!"
"Fuuuuuuuuccccckkkkk"
"Ooowwwwww oh god it hurts soooooo baaaaaaaaad"

Half a mile away from my campsite, I passed through a tiny hamlet of houses, there was still one more deep valley and one more massive hill climb to do. I stopped in the shade of one of the houses, bending over my walking poles, my vision was starting to go hazy, my body swaying about to keel over. The road and the houses blurred around me. Was it the heat waves? Or was I about to-

"Goodness... are you alright there? Do you need a doctor?" this came from a middle aged lady walking her small dog, she'd stopped briefly to chat to a man polishing his BMW outside his house. They were looking at me with grave concern.

"Oh... hi... I'm ok, I just need to rest a while... I'm hoping to get to North Morte campsite but I'm not sure I'll make it." I mumble something along those lines although I'm not entirely sure that's what I said.

"Gosh you poor thing, hiking in this heat! Would you like me to drive you there? North Morte's not far away but you've got a bloody big hill to climb before you get there." she says.

"Oh yes please... If it's not too much trouble... I hope I'm not interrupting your dog-walk! I can't take another step today... Thank you so much!"

"Alright wait here in the shade, I'm just walking home now anyway, my car's only a few houses away! I'm Jo, by the way."

Another angel in a car giving me a lift to my campsite, I thought, thank you universe! Jo drove me up to North Morte campsite just outside Woolacombe, I was struck again by how kind everyone I've met on this path has been to me so far and I felt a huge wave of gratitude wash over me. Despite spending most of the day in a mental fog of anger and frustration, the fog cleared in that car with Jo and I felt so thankful that I was here on this path having the most amazing adventure. How many people in their lives get to do this? I thought.

As we were nearing the campsite, my phone started ringing.

"Indy-pops! Are you ok? Are you hurt? I can see on the tracker you're going really fast? Why are you travelling at 30mph? What happened?" Dad said in a panic. Just before I left on this trip we'd downloaded a tracker on my phone so he could keep an eye on my progress. He'd obviously been checking it obsessively and got worried when he saw I was travelling at a pace of thirty miles an hour and not two.

"Haha Dad I'm fine. I've just hitched a lift from a nice local lady called Jo. She's driving me to North Morte - we're about two minutes away." I said, smiling over at Jo in the driver's seat who gave a knowing chuckle back.

"Oh thank goodness. I thought you were being kidnapped, or in an ambulance or something!" he said, breathing a huge sigh of relief.

"No, no, everything's fine. I'll call you back when I've set up camp ok? I love you."

"Ok my darling, love you too."

"Haha, I know that feeling. No matter how old they get you'll always worry about your kids. I'm the same with my sons!" Jo said with a wry smile.

At North Morte, basking in the early evening sun outside my tent with my sore legs stretched out in front of me, I called my family to check in with them and updated them on how I was doing. Before I started my walk, I was stubborn and convinced myself that I could do six weeks of hiking with no rest days and no help, 15 miles a day, all by myself. My beloved path had humbled me, and I realised that I was going to need rest days, and I was going to need help. I simply didn't have the strength to carry more than a week's worth of food. And the food I was carrying wasn't even enough to nourish my weakening body. My Dad, being the protective worrier he is, immediately said, "Right! I'm coming up tomorrow and bringing you home for a rest day! Ind, you can't do this by yourself, my love, ok? Me and your Mum will come up every week and do resupply trips for you, we'll sort this out don't you worry, you can do this, you just need to accept help, ok?"

I couldn't argue with him, I knew he was right, but I couldn't help but feel a little deflated that I did need help... but then I am not a superhuman - my body has limits! And I felt so thankful to have such a wonderful support team who lived so close by, it seemed silly to not have help when we all LIVE in this same area.

I'd just finished chatting to my family when Alastair, George & Aaron turned up at the campsite.

"Hey! You made it!" I said, excited to see familiar faces.

"Hey! You did too, well done! Corrr, it was a tough one today wasn't it?" George said, surprised.

"Yeah, my legs are really suffering... going to head over for a long shower in a minute." I replied, gesturing to my legs which suddenly didn't feel attached to my body and had now gone completely numb.

"Well, we're going to do the same and then head into Woolacombe for dinner - would you like to come with us? It'd be cool to get to know you, you look like you could use a hearty meal as well!" said Alastair.

"Aw that'd be really cool, I'd love to, give me a shout when you're ready!" I said, blushing with a girlish excitement at the thought of being taken out to dinner by three handsome men.

And with that, I raced to the shower block and tried to make myself as presentable as possible, did my routine of massaging my aching body in the shower, washing and brushing my mane of now sunkissed, unruly hair, slapping some moisturiser on my face, desperately swiping deodorant all over my underarms and putting on my clean pair of yoga leggings, a bottle green t-shirt and my turquoise camp sandals. I stared at myself in the mirror, not exactly dressed for a dinner date, but it'll have to do.

As I came out of the shower block, I bumped into Aaron coming out of the men's showers.

"We've been talking about you today, it's so amazing how you're doing this on your own! You're so tiny, how do you do it with that pack on?!" he said.

"I've been talking to myself a lot, that helps. But honestly I'm finding it so hard... and if I think about how much I have left to do, it gets too overwhelming so I just try to take it one step at a time, literally! And I hitchhiked the last half a mile here, I couldn't do another step today!" I admitted.

"Ahhh, you little cheater! You're not supposed to get lifts!" he gasped in mock jest, gently nudging my shoulder with his.

"No but seriously, you're doing great, don't beat yourself up about getting help here and there, you still have a long journey ahead." he added.

The four of us got a taxi into Woolacombe and went for dinner at Brundle's restaurant right next to the beach. It was such a lovely evening laughing, sharing stories and getting to know my three new friends. I felt a little sad that it was their last night and I wouldn't be seeing them again on this path. We watched the golden red sun set over the calm sea together and I chuckled to myself at how romantic this would be if it was a date with one guy, but I got to do it with three!

Back at camp I said goodbye to my three handsome dates and snuggled up into bed, the angry thoughts of the day seeming like someone else's thoughts from a distant galaxy.

Day six. Dad brought me home for a rest day. The journey home was a bitter pill to swallow. I didn't want to go home, I wanted to carry on, but I knew I *needed* to go home. When I woke up that morning, my calves felt like they were developing an injury. As soon as we walked through the door Dad started feeding me with all the food in the entire world, so determined was he that he would heal his little girl and she was not going to go hungry or suffer. We also went through my backpack and had a strict cull of anything that I wasn't using and didn't need. I made the decision that taking three of each clothing item was not necessary. I would take the one set of clothes I was wearing, one spare pair of socks and one spare pair of knickers and that would be it. I got rid of the camping lantern, the multi-tool knife, my swimsuit and some highly unnecessary first aid items (why did I think I'd need a fire blanket?) and eventually we got my pack weight down to 16kg - SO much better!

I ran myself a bath after feasting and oh. my. goodness. It was an exquisite experience. It felt so good yet so painful at the same time to sink my body into the hot soothing water. I could actually feel the stiffness in my muscles melt away. The friction burns on my shoulders and lower back stinged at first contact with the water, the blisters on my feet throbbed, and then - bliss...

I mused in the bath about my journey so far, I'd walked almost 50 miles in five days and I felt really proud of myself. There was still such a long way to go and even though it had been so incredibly hard so far, the trail was calling to me. She was saying, "come back to me, India. We belong together". I couldn't wait to return to her, it was like an addiction, a primal craving to be with her. My true love. My heart's desire. Being away from her felt weird... like I was missing a limb... or missing a purpose.

So often in life, we just bumble through, not thinking, not feeling, like zombies on a hamster wheel. Wake up, go to work, come back to the box we live in, stare at a little blue rectangle for a while, sleep, repeat. It's only when you truly place yourself outside of your comfort zone that you have no choice but to face every part of yourself, feel every emotion and make peace with your shadows. This is what being on the SWCP was like. She thrusts you inward and forces you to become integrated with the parts of yourself that perhaps you have been subconsciously trying to avoid all your life. For me, it was accepting my anger. As women, especially growing up in a religion, we are taught that we shouldn't feel such vulgarity as anger. We should only be soft and submissive and be the person that everyone turns to to feel better.

But here's the thing: anger is a healthy part of being human when used in a productive way. Anger lives within all of us. And it's only because society views it as a bad thing, that it then bursts out uncontrollably from time to time and causes serious damage in ways such as domestic violence, crime, even terrorism. If we all made peace with our inner anger, and utilised it in a healthy way to do good, to improve ourselves both as individuals and as a collective... Wow, what a bright future that would be.

On my journey so far, I had felt deeply every wave of anger. Anger at the physical pain I was in, anger at the relentless ups and downs of the terrain, anger at the traumas of the past few years. But instead of letting it overwhelm me, I harnessed it in a healthy way that pushed me forward. I felt the wave deeply, surfing it as it swelled, then crashed, then ebbed away in its natural life cycle. And beyond that lie soaring highs of emotion: complete rapture and gratitude at the abundance of life. The wholeness of being an awakened soul on this adventure that was growing and healing me exponentially.

My home life growing up in West Byfleet in the 90s had always been incredibly loving. It was a simple life. Innocent, scarce in material luxuries, yet overflowing with the unconditional love of my parents and my brother, two years my junior.

It was a frugal and sheltered upbringing, however, because everyone in our family, including us four, all my grandparents, aunts, uncles, cousins etc, were Jehovah's Witnesses. Being a JW felt totally normal and totally alien at the same time. It was all I knew, and yet I knew it had to not be all there is. Every Thursday and Sunday we'd go to the Kingdom Hall for meetings with our local congregation and we'd be expected to contribute both financially and with our time knocking on non-believers' doors preaching "the Truth". We'd regularly have abuse shouted at us from the residents who did not want to be preached at. We were not allowed to celebrate anything but Jehovah Himself; no birthdays, no Christmas, no Easter, no Valentine's etc, and it was frowned upon to indulge in materialism.

There was very much a hierarchy - Jehovah the Creator (God) at the top, then men second, then women & children at the bottom. We were frequently reminded of this at meetings, weddings and all throughout the bible. The group of older men, or "elders" as they were officially called, would all sit in a group together on a platform at the front of the Kingdom Hall (JW's version of a church) whilst the women and children would sit at the back. The sole role of a woman was at home, to serve her husband and bear him heirs. Submit, serve, sacrifice. Eve was apparently created from Adam's rib after all...

I struggled to engage with these beliefs, but I knew of no other existence and for the first 12 years of my life I felt loved, secure and safe. Yes, the stories in the bible frightened me. Yes, there was a constant anxiety of burning in hell for all eternity if ever I did anything deemed to be a "sin". And yes, it was a strict and judgmental environment. But I had the love of my parents and my brother and that was enough for me. I'd loved growing up with my little brother by my side. B is a handsome, creative, funny, intelligent man now and I have such fond memories of playing in the street outside our home as kids, digging up woodlice, climbing trees and making entire kingdoms out of Lego.

We moved to rural Devon when I was eight years old and found a new congregation. I made some great pals in the local primary school who weren't JWs so it was rather a novelty to suddenly have "normal" friends, as it was frowned upon to socialise outside of the congregation. It was then that I started to suspect something uneasy, that life was changing, but I couldn't put my finger on how.

Then four years later, at age 12, my parents divorced. It wasn't a huge surprise as I'd noticed them arguing secretly for the past couple of years. But what did come as a shock was the complete life change that followed. All of a sudden my parents, my brother and I were shunned from our family and congregation. Cast

out as sinners, the black sheep.
"De-Fellowshipped" is the official term.

As a hormonal young girl, just entering her teen years, I couldn't understand how our family could just abandon us like that, just when we really needed them. My family was breaking and where was my community? They'd disappeared, given up on us. We were no longer JWs, I had no one to turn to who could truly understand, and it felt like I had to completely relearn what life was, how to act, how to be... WHAT to be. I was grateful for the friends I had made in secondary school by then, but they couldn't possibly understand what coming out of what was essentially a cult was like. We'd lost money in the divorce, not that we had much to begin with anyway. Sometimes all that Mum could afford to feed my brother and I was a tin of tomato soup mixed with some pasta. But she did her very best. There was always something warm to eat at the end of the day. And an infinite amount of warm cuddles and kisses at bedtime.

In my mid 20's we reconnected with my Mum's side of the family and they became more accepting of our differences. We have a mutual respect and understanding for each other now. But my Dad's relatives I haven't heard from or spoken to since the divorce. It's sad but I've come to realise that if people can so easily give up on you like that, even if they are your family, then it's not worth pursuing a relationship that was never authentic in the first place. All the family I ever need is with my parents, my brothers and my close friends.

I have respect for people that choose to live by a religion. Everyone has their own unique values and beliefs and as long as they aren't causing harm to others then that's great for them. But in my experience, there is a dark side of religion that is rife with hate, hypocrisy, judgement and wounded masculine/feminine energy. The elders would make up all these commandments we had to live by, but in secret, in the sordid pits behind closed doors, they'd be abusing the very rules they created. And the women and children that followed them out of fear.

I do believe there is a higher power. I wouldn't call it "God". That word has too many connotations. Some may say "source", or the "universe", or "spirit". To be honest, I'm not sure what I'd call it, but I feel it is there, guiding us to where we're meant to be. It is pure. Without judgement. It is love. And it's only through the hands of a few malicious humans that the message has been corrupted to control others.

Day seven on the SWCP and I felt much restored after my rest day, I was itching to get back to my beloved path. Mum drove me back to Woolacombe where from there it was an easy, flat and varied walk through a golf course, a military training ground and finally the beautiful

Braunton nature reserve. I annoyed a couple of golfers by getting in their way, but apart from that it was a very satisfying 14 mile day - my best yet! I felt so relieved that it was an easier day, my legs were still in a great deal of pain, but at least the terrain was so much easier. Once I reached Braunton town at the other end, I decided that I wanted to bypass the inland estuary route around Bideford and Barnstaple and go straight to Westward Ho! (yes, the exclamation point is part of the name) which was just 50 yards across the estuary from Braunton. It would take me an extra two days to walk around the estuary and it just seemed a bit pointless and disheartening even though it was technically part of the official route. But by this point at the end of the day I was in so much pain again and didn't care one iota about walking around a suburban estuary.

I felt content at the time saved as I set up wild camp just outside of Westward Ho! on a beautiful grassy verge right next to the path overlooking the setting sun over the ocean. I breathed deep as the clean air soothed my lungs, the dappled pink hues of sunset inviting my vision to relax and the sounds of the lapping waves a sweet summer lament. I had just completed my first week of hiking the SWCP. I felt so proud of myself and so excited for the fresh adventures yet to be uncovered.

Week 2 – Pain

Day eight. My little Turtle Tent is struggling. As I packed it away this morning I noticed the bendy poles are starting to crack and break quite badly. I don't know why I was surprised as the poor thing isn't built to be put up and taken down every day - it's a £20 pop up tent that you'd use a couple times at a festival, not on a long distance backpacking hiking adventure.

Today's route was another tough uphill-downhill struggle. The path hugged the rugged black cliff-edges with the jagged crashing waves below and I clutched my walking poles like my life depended on them. Which, actually, it did. For most of its 630 mile length, the SWCP is just 30cm wide and very overgrown with grasses and shrubs that seem determined to trip you up every step. I battled through the foliage, pushing through narrow tunnels of hedges that scraped the sides of my already battered tent that was still bungee-strapped to the outside of my pack. My face became filthy with cobwebs, grass seeds, dirt and scratches, I swear I could physically see a hum of odour emanating from my skin.

I wailed and swore and growled like a rabid dog, "why isn't this getting any easier?!?!" I cried. It was such slow progress, but finally, there, a couple miles in the distance, I could see the little fishing village of Clovelly. My finish-line for the day.

I'd read about Clovelly in the SWCP guidebook, it seemed a very interesting place. A village that was part of a massive estate privately owned by the very wealthy son of an Earl. All the residents of the village rent from him. It reminded me of the village in that film with Simon Pegg - Hot Fuzz. There was a hostel there that I'd hoped to stay in as it didn't seem like the kind of place one could wild-camp and I didn't want to disrespect the landowner or get into trouble.

At last, after 11 miles, I'd reached Clovelly! I was exhausted, filthy, pissed off, absolutely starving and looking forward to a shower. But what greeted me was not what I'd expected - you have to pay to get into the village. What?! So I'm going to pay to stay in a hostel but I also have to pay £7 just to bloody walk a hundred feet to get there?! I was living off the small nest-egg of savings I'd built up over the past couple years and felt resentful that it was now dwindling away.

I reluctantly paid the entrance fee and started to make my way down to the hostel. It was an incredibly steep downhill pebble track and it took all the strength in my thighs to keep my balance and stop myself from slipping. The weather that day had been cloudy and mild, but the sun had come out for the evening now and it was getting hot. Red-faced tourists making their way back up the cobbled road panted and struggled their way past me. We exchange withering, knowing looks.

Oh... Okaaaaayyy... The hostel is a building site. It's closed. Fuck sake could this day get any more frustrating?! I thought. Where am I supposed to stay now?! I swallowed back angry tears at the thought of walking back up the steep road, away from Clovelly to find somewhere to wild-camp and wasting the entrance fee I'd just paid. But just opposite the street from the building-site-hostel was the New Inn. It looked rather fancy and I approached it with trepidation at the reality of my depleting finances.

"Hi there... um... I'm hiking the coast path for charity... I had hoped to stay in that hostel opposite the street tonight... but it seems to be closed?" I say to the New Inn receptionist, trying my best to seem polite and not the red hot fire of wild anger I was feeling inside.
"Hello! Welcome to Clovelly! Yes, I'm sorry, we run the hostel as well and it is indeed closed for a refurb at the moment. We have a single room available here tonight if you need somewhere to stay? Breakfast is included as well." The receptionist said. She had a calm, kind face, a genuine smile that made me feel at ease and I started to relax a little in her presence.

"Oh thank you that would be so amazing... but I can't really afford it... how much is it?"
"Well our standard rate is £120 per night..." *gulp*
"...But as you're on your own and it's last minute, I can squeeze you into our small single room for £60? Our hostel rate is £20 per night, so that is the best I can do I'm afraid."
I didn't need to think about it, her kindness moved me so much, I took the room happily.

It was a beautiful room, just about big enough for a single bed with an en-suite bathroom, cream carpets, cream curtains and fresh white bed linen. I tip-toed around, super aware that I was filthy and didn't want to get the pristinely clean room dirty. I peeled my crusty, sweat stained clothes off and hopped in the shower with my underwear and socks still on - they were oddly reeking of decay so I thought it would be a good idea to wash them as well as myself.

Ahhhh. Clean, warm water. Shampoo! Conditioner! What luxury! The little freebie mini bottles in the bathroom were like nuggets of gold to me. I relished using every last drop of them in that shower. The water that ran off me and my underwear was dish-water brown mixed with bits of foliage and droplets of dried blood from the scratches all over my body. I looked like I'd been mauled by a gang of cats.

Once out of the shower, I wondered what I might do for dinner. I had my rations, of course, but I wondered if it would be safe to fire up my camping stove in this tiny room with a smoke alarm on the ceiling right above the bed... I pondered this dilemma for a while and eventually came to the inevitable conclusion that I would have to eat the rations cold. Straight from the packet. I sat naked, cross-legged on the bed and ate my veggie potato curry straight from the vac-pac pouch followed by a granola bar - the scene looked so pathetic I actually roared with laughter. And of course, I was still ravenously hungry afterwards.

Day nine. The morning sunrise gently dappled its way through the cream curtains of my single room at the New Inn. I awoke feeling so well rested. The soft, clean bed was heavenly to sleep on and it made me appreciate it so much more after sleeping on hard ground under canvas for the past week and a half. I'd slept naked so as not to get the sheets dirty with my clothes so it was rather a disappointment to then shove myself into the now cardboard-stiff layers. At least my underwear and socks which had been drying on the towel radiator overnight were now clean.

Breakfast at the New Inn was enormous, and I gobbled it all up as if someone would snatch it away. Local handmade sausages and bacon, thick crusty toast, mushrooms, beans, tomato, silky scrambled eggs. I even managed to squeeze in a bowl of granola before it all hit my stomach at once and I felt a bit sick. But in the most glorious way.

The route out of Clovelly passed through the beautiful grounds of the estate, ancient woodlands of old gnarly trees and exquisite wildflowers everywhere I looked in shades of yellow and fuschia. That led onto more dramatic stretches of rugged coastline with unusual rock formations that looked like statues of some ancient fearsome creatures and then onto farmland of lush green tall crops that danced about in the summer breeze.

The weather was sunny and warm and the 11 miles I achieved before reaching Hartland Quay seemed to pass by in a flash. I felt so much stronger than I did at the start of my journey and my pack was feeling so much lighter after the cull of unneeded things. Something was brewing, however. Something that I was too afraid to draw attention to. I'd been developing a slight limp in my left foot for the past few days. I didn't want to think about it. I couldn't say it outloud otherwise it would then be true. Nope. The best thing to do is just ignore it, I tried to convince myself.

I met up with Dad at Hartland Quay for a resupply and he did his usual of fussing over me, feeding me with a ton of stuff he'd brought in a coolbox and worrying about where I would sleep tonight. I looked at him and just swelled with love and gratitude. He'd had a difficult start to this year too. A couple weeks after I'd left my ex in January and moved in with him, Dad found out that he'd got cancer. Throughout the last few months of 2020, he'd felt unusually drained of energy, which, if you know my Dad, is very strange for him. He's always had such a zest for life and a strength that amazed me even as he approached his 60s. But a few months ago he'd developed a urinary tract infection that wouldn't go away, and it just seemed to drain the energy out of him.

And then it came. The word that carries so much fear. Cancer. In the lymph nodes in his groin. Thankfully, the doctors had caught it early and they were able to get it out of him as soon as possible in February of this year. I'm so grateful for them and I don't like to think about what might've happened if they hadn't caught it so soon. Dad is my anchor. Every time I've struggled in life, he's been there to scoop me up. He always knows what to say to make things better. And as I looked at him at Hartland Quay excitedly shoving homemade brownies into my mouth, the colour back in his cheeks, the twinkle back in his eye, I vowed to never take him for granted.

Not long after my parents divorced, he'd met a wonderful woman, my step-mum, fallen in love and they'd had two sons together, my youngest brothers. J, in his late teens now, is an incredibly talented musician. The bass guitarist in a rock band with his mates, they're incredibly charismatic and on the brink of stardom, I just know it! M, twenty years younger than me, and a ball of energy. Very bright, inquisitive and just pure adorable joy. I'm so glad Dad found happiness and contentment and it's almost hard to remember life without my crazy little bro's. I don't see them as "half-brothers". They're my full brothers. That's that and I love them as such.

"Indy-pops, I've had a little scout around the local area of places you could camp tonight. The six miles from here to Morwenstow is severe according to the guide book. I'm worried you're not strong enough yet to do all the steep valley and cliff climbs coming up. It's relentless. It's one after the other. And there's heavy rain on the way and I'm worried the path is going to get very slippery. So, here's my suggestion: there's a pub at Morwenstow that'll let you camp in their garden tonight. How about I take you there now, skip these next six miles and we can come back during one of your rest days in a couple week's time when you're stronger and finish it?" he said. I could see the anxiety in his eyes. I just knew he was still obsessively checking the tracking app we'd downloaded onto our phones everyday to see that I was still, in fact, alive.

I was torn. I didn't want to skip bits. I wasn't a purist thru-hiker by any means, but I wanted to do this properly. Yet, I also didn't want to cause unnecessary stress for my Dad - he was still technically in the recovery stage of his surgery even though he insisted he was back to normal. So I agreed.

"Ok Dad, thank you, that's a good idea. We'll come back in a couple week's time." I said, trying to seem jovial and not let my disappointment show.

Dad drove me to Morwenstow, a quintessentially quaint little country village complete with thatched cottages and a chintzy tea room, we gave each other a big bear-hug goodbye and I went into the The Bush Inn to ask if I could camp in their garden for the night. I promised to buy a meal from them in return and the lovely staff there were only too happy to accommodate me. I had a massive dinner of a gourmet halloumi burger, skinny fries, red cabbage slaw and sweet chilli sauce - it was SO. GOOD. Oh my goodness, I devoured every mouthful and felt incredibly sleepy afterwards. A full-on food coma. I chatted to the couple sitting next to me having a dinner date.

"Oh you must've read The Salt Path?!" said the lady excitedly after I told her what I was doing. This made me chuckle. I'd passed many tourists on the SWCP already, being the height of the summer season, and every single one of them had asked whether I'd read The Salt Path. It's a book about a couple who had also walked the South West Coast Path and I'd never heard of it before, but everyone I'd met so far had waxed lyrical about it. So much so that I probably didn't need to read it - I heard the story so many times already through the mouths of the tourists. I'll read it when I get back and compare notes, I thought.

I awoke on my tenth day with the murky light of dawn. I'd had a comfortable night's sleep in the soft grassy garden of The Bush Inn and this morning the air was thick with mist, the grass heavy and sagging with dew. It was chilly and I could smell rain on the horizon so I quickly packed up my things and got going. I left the shelter of the village and rejoined the coast path just a few hundred metres away to swirling winds and short sharp rain showers.

"WOOOOOOHHOOOOHAAAOOOO!!" it was all I could do to howl like a wolf again and become one with my inner wild. I was thriving today. The wind was whipping, the rain was lashing and I was yomping up and down the valleys to Bude like a stormtrooper. I LOVE walking in the rain, it brings out my inner wild-woman. There's something I just find so sensual about being that connected with nature. The cool, wet rain falling on my hot skin and then rising back up as steam, the wind caressing my face and ruffling through my tangled hair like a passionate lover, my hands running through the long grasses, the smell of wet foliage. I felt like Kate Bush in her Wuthering Heights music video, all I needed to complete the scene was a floaty red dress. The weight of my pack didn't seem so heavy today as my spirit was invigorated by the elements.

I walked past a bizarre government communications facility called GCHQ. It's basically a field with these gigantic satellite dishes scattered about that look like something out of a sci-fi film. I joked to myself that they were probably spying on us from there, or communicating with aliens or something...

After an exhilarating rollercoaster of nine miles, I reached Upper Lynstone campsite just outside Bude and decided that's where I'd stop for the day. It was a pretty luxurious campsite that even had laundry facilities which I jumped at the chance to use. Of course, as I only had one set of clothes I had to hang out in the laundry room wearing only my waterproofs as my clothes went through the washing machine and then the tumble dryer. Oh, it felt so good to be able to put on clean, warm, dry clothes! The rain was coming down pretty heavily then so I dived back to my tent and snuggled in for the evening. I had to eat my ration meal cold straight from the packet again, but that didn't bother me this time, I was feeling strong, fulfilled and satisfied from the day. It finally seemed like this path was getting a little easier. The pain in my foot from a couple days ago had subsided and I felt like I was really getting into my stride now.

Pitter-patter-pitter-patter. The rain falling on my tent started lulling me to sleep. The ground at this campsite was incredibly hard but I tried my best to find a comfy position and get a good night sleep in, I wanted to continue this momentum.

Day eleven. I woke up feeling very groggy after a restless night trying to get comfy on such hard ground. I probably only got a couple hours sleep in total here and there, dipping in and out of consciousness. But I cracked on with the day nonetheless. The rain had subsided overnight and the weather this morning was overcast with the smell of rain still lingering in the cool air.

The path from Bude was challenging but beautiful. More steep cliffs and valleys and views of the sweeping sandy beaches that are so abundant in that area. I was struggling up a particularly steep valley, pausing often to catch my breath and trying to ignore the pain that was starting to return to my left foot. On my way up I passed through an enchanted forest. It was so peaceful with a bubbling stream running through, gnarly tangled trees, birds singing and wild flowers carpeting the forest floor. I stopped for a while to soak in the atmosphere.

Then, something truly magical happened. Climbing out of that forest and up into the clouds, at the top of the cliff stood a small thicket of stunted oak trees. Stunted oak trees

are very old, short in stature with a wide reach of
twisting branches. And in the middle of this
gathering was the most beautiful oak tree I have
ever seen. All the other trees circled around her
as if she were an ancient goddess they
worshipped, Mother Nature personified.

She spoke to me. She drew me in and my
instincts just took over. I went to her as if in a
trance and put my arms around her thick mossy
trunk, her low hanging limbs draping around my
head, returning the embrace. I hugged her close
and I could feel her life-force, her sacred energy
pulsating so powerfully around us. I knew at that
moment that my soul was meant to find this
tree.

As a teenager, I believed in the magic of the
forest, in fairies, folklore and the energy of
Mother Earth. But in my 20s I had allowed that
knowing to be stolen from me. I had lost my way,
I had lost my wonder. But as I was hugging my
soul-tree, that knowing came rushing back to
me. I weeped with happiness in her embrace, I
leant my face into her soft mossy bark and I
knew that the fairies that lived in this thicket
were watching over us, guiding me with their
love and light.

I don't know how long I was there hugging my
soul-tree. Time just seemed to slip away and it
felt like I had become one with her. Her bark had

become my skin, her mossy branches became my hair, her roots intertwined with my toes.

The rest of the route to Crackington Haven, I walked in a blissful daze and that night in my tent I slept so soundly. Something had changed profoundly within me that day. A shift in my soul so seismic, yet so quiet that to a passer-by it would be barely noticeable. But to me, I knew I would never be the same again. I couldn't quite put into words what that shift was, but it was there, it was real, it was wonderful, and suddenly I didn't feel so much pain in my heart anymore.

Day twelve and today, Mother Earth was with me in abundance. My journey so far had, for the majority of the time, been a fog of pain, blood, sweat, tears and frustration. But since my magical experience yesterday, it's like my eyes had been washed anew and I was seeing this path for the first time. Wildflowers of gerbera daisies, foxgloves, cow parsley, buttercups, chicory and so many thrifts spilled from the path in a celebration of colour. I hiked through lots more valleys and cliffs but this time with not one, but TWO cascading waterfalls! The sun was shining, the sky and the ocean mirrored each other in a competition to see who could be the bluest. It really was an utter joy to behold such exquisite beauty. I felt humbled and privileged to witness it, to be a part of it.

Approaching the ancient town of Tintagel, I picked my way through an unusual valley of rock formations that looked like something out of Lord of The Rings with tall columns and sheer drops of charcoal grey rock, cut through by a slice of gushing river. Finally reaching Tintagel after 11 miles of walking that day, I did feel pretty knackered. The twinge in my left foot was starting to bother me. I willed it to go away. I didn't want to say the "i" word (injury). I couldn't, I WOULDN'T fall injured. I ignored the stone of unrest forming in my stomach and met up with Mum for a resupply and an upgrade of my tent. My poor little turtle tent had finally given up. The poles had a complete breakage and it was now a collapsed heap of fabric and jagged spikes.

I set up camp next to her motorhome in a field behind a carpark in Tintagel in my shiny new khaki coloured tent from Mountain Warehouse that was made specifically for backpacking. It was super light and packed away neatly into a small bag that, hallelujah, fit into my pack! No more looking like a Teenage Mutant Ninja Turtle! No more swaying in the winds about to fly off a cliff-face! I felt so much better balanced wearing my pack now.

That evening, Mum and I went for an amazing pub dinner and to the big surprise for both of us, I had... wait for it... a steak and ale pie! Normally this dish would repulse me. I've never liked the taste of red meat or beer. But this path just makes me crave all the foods, especially the heavier stuff that normally would make my digestive system explode. My body was just constantly burning off everything I was consuming - I needed those heavier foods to give me the energy to do this.

After dinner, we got back to the car park and settled down for the evening. The grassy field behind it where I pitched my tent was lovely and soft and I fell asleep quickly. My heart and soul was still glowing from the encounter with my soul tree yesterday. It felt like finally I was starting to get into a proper stride.

I said goodbye once again to my loving, supportive Mum on the morning of my thirteenth day and set off on the 14 mile stretch to Polzeath. It was another tough day in sweltering hot sunshine with so many valleys and cliff climbs again. I wondered if this relentless rollercoaster terrain would ever end. Up and down, up and down, up and down constantly. There must've been a half marathon race on as I stopped often to allow runners to pass. They looked utterly knackered running up and down those steep valleys in this blistering heat. I felt their pain.

Passing through the famous Port Isaac, I stopped for a blissful ice cream and watched the throng of tourists sweatily jostling amongst the tiny streets of this old fishing village. It was rather a culture shock to be amongst so many people again, so accustomed was I now to being in the wild on my own.

Eating that ice cream on the side of the street outside the famous Golden Lion pub, with my one set of clothes, my faithful companion with all my survival essentials strapped to my back and watching civilization shuffle by, I felt every inch the outsider. Big, shiny, posh Range Rovers angrily beeped their horns and fought for parking spaces like hippopotamuses fighting over a watering hole. Red faces in camel coloured slacks & polo shirts and glamorous ladies in ostentatious wide brim hats & paisley print maxi dresses shoved past each other in a competition to see who could get the best selfie for their Instagram page.

And I stood to the side, an observer, a lone she-wolf, answering to no one, trying to prove herself to no one, deeply content, a lioness watching over her queendom.

I carried on trying to ignore the small fire burning in my left foot. It felt ok once I got into my stride, I just had to keep going. "Don't stop, India" I said to myself. "Keep moving, keep going, it'll be fine" I said to myself out loud. If I said it would be fine out loud then it would be fine... wouldn't it?

I finally reached Southwinds campsite at Polzeath, exhausted, sweaty and hungry as usual. It's a cute little family run campsite right near the path with beautiful views out to the sparkling blue sea. I'd met two couples at separate points during the day, one in their 30s called Gemma & Adam from the New Forest and the other in their 50s called Phil & Lorraine from Dorset. Both couples were hiking the entire SWCP in one go like I was and they both turned up at Southwinds! We all camped together and spent the evening getting to know each other and sharing stories of our journeys so far.

Gemma worked as a physio in the NHS and had had a nightmare of a year working during the pandemic. So she and fiancé Adam (who had travelled all over the world and had some really fascinating stories) decided that they needed a break before they got married, and what better way to do it hiking the SWCP! Phil & Lorraine were a couple of tattooed bikers that at first glance were a bit intimidating looking, but were actually big softies. They had decided to sell up everything and go off on an adventure. They'd been finding the physical side of things really difficult as they weren't in the best of shape, they said. Lorraine was suffering with some horrific looking blisters all over her feet. I thought they were doing amazing and was full of admiration for them.

The sun began to set on a very satisfying day as I said goodnight to my new friends and curled up in my tent for the night. My body felt achy and tired, but my heart and soul felt so content at being on this path. It was quickly becoming my home and I couldn't imagine a life before, or a life after. It was everything. It was all things. My beloved path had consumed me into her bubble and I never wanted it to end.

Day 14, my two week SWCP anniversary! It was a baking hot day, not a cloud in sight, and I woke up feeling eager to get started on another day's hiking. My body however, had other ideas. The pain in my left foot was becoming harder and harder to ignore. Every step I winced as the feeling of a sharp knife shot through my foot and up my leg.

"Shit, India... Ok... Well... It's Sunday. Maybe I'll just walk four miles to Padstow then rest for the day. Just take it slow." I said to myself. It was such a hot day as well that I knew I wouldn't have the energy to walk much in such oppressive heat.

So, I set off in the already unbearable heat at 9am and walked at a snail's pace to Padstow. It was excruciating. I tried my best to walk evenly and steadily, I didn't want to overcompensate on my stronger foot and get that one injured as well, but the heat, the weight of my pack, and crossing the relentlessly undulating soft sand dunes between Polzeath and Padstow, had me limping for most of the way.

I got to the ferry crossing to Padstow at midday and bumped into Phil & Lorraine catching the same ferry.
"India! Oh god, it's too hot today. How are you coping? We've booked an Airb'n'b in Padstow for today and are going to chill out for the rest of the day. My feet are on fire!!" said Lorraine.
"Hey guys, not so good, my foot isn't doing too well. I'm gunna stop in Padstow today as well. I'll see you at some point on the path tomorrow no doubt!"

We got off the ferry at Padstow and I said goodbye to my friends as they dashed into Mountain Warehouse to replace various lost and broken pieces of kit. I slowly limped my way upstream through the docks and along a picturesque riverside path to Dennis Cove campsite - a lovely spot nestled amongst the wooded hills of the River Camel estuary. But I was limping so badly at this point that I struggled to walk even with the support of my poles. I quickly put my tent up like a well choreographed military operation and limp-marched my way to the shower block - ahhhhh that feeling never gets old. The feeling of running water on salty, dirty, weather-beaten skin.

I spent the rest of the baking hot day in the shade of my tent, massaging my feet and legs, trying to work out the kinks in the muscles, dozing on and off and just trying not to put any weight at all on my feet. A lovely kind middle aged couple in their converted campervan parked up beside my tent and fed me a delicious cup of sweet tea after I told them what I was doing.

Everyday on this path I was humbled by the human kindness I'd experienced. As much as I had to take precautions as a young solo female traveller (case in point: self defence spray, whistle and multi-tool knife), I also felt totally safe and eternally grateful for the endless cups of tea I'd been offered throughout my journey so far. There's something about a good old-fashioned, classic cup of British builder's tea. Perhaps it's just built into the DNA of us Brits. But to be offered a cup of tea is like someone giving you a big hug, saying it's ok, you are loved, you are supported, you are cared for. It means something. It makes any situation feel that little bit more bearable.

Early evening came and, surprise surprise, I was ravenous. Still ravenous after I'd cooked up a portion of veggie sausages and beans. My foot was feeling a little better after all the massaging I'd done throughout the day and so I thought, well, I'm in Padstow: I've gotta sample some of Rick's fish and chips! Rick Stein practically owns Padstow. The legendary celebrity chef, with his comforting dulcet tones and passion for seafood, was someone I grew up watching on the telly and is synonymous with this area. So I carefully strolled back into town, still limping a little, but very much led by the rumbling in my stomach. The smell hit me first. Salt. Vinegar. Batter scraps. Warm newspaper. My mouth was salivating as I queued up at Rick's chippy on the riverside.

I excitedly carried my bag of scampi & chips as if it was a bag of precious gemstones to the harbour and found a park bench to sit on to enjoy the ritual I was about to partake in. Eating had become just that - a sacred ritualistic part of every day. If I wasn't thinking about walking, I was thinking about my next meal. Everytime I put something in my mouth it was like I was eating for the first time. Rapturous. Sweet relief from my stomach at having some sustenance to fuel my demanding body with. My taste buds had become even more receptive to flavour being on this journey. Even the humble chip was an explosion of ecstasy and joy.

Beady black eyes with greedy yellow beaks eyed me up from a few feet away. And I gave them the beady eyes back.
"Not today, seagulls. You're barking up the wrong tree with me." I said to them.
I think they got the message that I wasn't to be messed with, not some blissfully unaware tourist that they could dive bomb.

As soon as my head hit the pillow back at the campsite, I was out for the count, briefly dreaming vividly of having chips for legs that seemed impossible to walk over sand on. I kept sinking and sinking into the sand... and then I had wings, my chip-legs tucked beneath me, soaring high above an ocean of tea... and then black.

Week 3 – Getting There

Day 15, the start of my third week on the SWCP.
My mornings were becoming a well-practised
routine of waking up with the sunrise, having my
breakfast protein shake with oats, nuts and
seeds mixed in, brush teeth, go to the loo, pack
everything away again into my backpack and set
off.

I had been struggling with breakfasts in the
early days of my walk. Me and porridge do not
get on. It's the texture, it just makes me gag, my
throat physically won't let me swallow it! Slimy
and gloopy and just... yuck. So what I found
works much better for me is to mix some of the
Vega chocolate flavoured multinutrient protein
powder I'd brought (highly highly recommend,
by the way) with plenty of water, a 50g sachet of
oats and nuts & seeds and have it as like a thick
shake. Much more palatable.

The path from Padstow was, to my relief, a lot
flatter than it had been recently. The weather
was cloudy and cool as well and, although my
foot was still in a lot of pain, it was a super
enjoyable 13 mile day. I passed the stunning
beaches lining the busy hotspots of Trevone and
Harlyn Bay and beautiful grassy headlands
sticking out into the wild of the Celtic Sea. I'd
bumped into Phil & Lorraine a couple times in
the morning and we exchanged warm hellos

and see-you-soons. That was another thing I was loving about long distance hiking - when you make friends, there's never a grieving final goodbye. It's always a "see you at some point down the path!"

As I got to Harlyn Bay, the path coming off the beach was not well sign-posted. I stood on the side of the road, at the entrance to a residential estate, at the other end of the beach staring at my map wondering which way to go. When I looked up I saw an incredibly handsome hiker, around my age, tall and athletic with ash-blonde short hair, also with a massive backpack on, and also staring at a map wondering which way to go. We instantly became friends. His name was Will, he was from London and was on a week long SWCP hiking trip from Westward Ho! to Newquay as a way to escape his stressful job and have a rethink of what he wanted from life. Kindred spirits.

We decided to walk the rest of the day together and it was actually a great help to walk with someone, talk and laugh and get to know each other as a way of distracting me from the pain in my foot. We eventually made it to Treyarnon Bay by mid afternoon and bumped into Phil & Lorraine again. As it turned out we had all planned to stay in the same campsite at Porthcothan so the four of us walked the rest of the way together to Carnevas Campsite.

It was a struggle for all of us. It was the end of a long day, we all had varying degrees of injury and it definitely felt like fate that we'd met up to walk these last few miles to the campsite together. We spurred each other on, cheered for each other and my heart swelled with love for my little SWCP family. I shared my last four squares of Kendal Mint Cake with them and that gave us a little bit of sugary rocket fuel to push out the final mile.

We staggered across the finish line into Carnevas together, exhausted but fulfilled like we were a team of olympic athletes, and set our tents next to each other. We all got an early night in, too tired for much more conversation, but with full hearts for what yet lay undiscovered in the tantalising prospects of tomorrow.

Day 16. Shit... shit fucking shit. There's no avoiding it now. No trying to ignore it anymore. My eyes filled with tears of pain and panic.

I'm injured.

No, no, no, no this can't happen!! I can't stop now!!

I've hobbled three miles from Porthcothan to Bedruthan Steps. Every step I've cried in excruciation. I had hoped to reach Newquay today, where I was meant to be meeting Dad again for a resupply, but there's no way that's happening. I can barely stand up, the pain in my left foot is like nothing I've ever felt before, like a burning hot poker stabbing through the outer muscle and shooting up my leg in a firework of pins and needles.

I sat on the bench outside the National Trust café at Bedruthan, head in my hands, crying on the phone to Dad who is parked up at Newquay waiting for me.

"Ok, ok Indy-pops, don't panic, my love. I'm coming to get you. I'll bring you home for a couple days."
"But I don't want to go home! What if this is it?! What if I can't finish?! What about all the charity money I've raised?!" I wailed like a stubborn child.

In the month leading up to my walk, I'd decided I would do it in aid of the charity Women's Aid and set up a fundraiser on the Just Giving website. Thankfully, I had not quite needed their services for my personal situation when I left my old life behind in January, but I wanted to do something to help the women and children in need who weren't as fortunate as me to have a support network around them. I'd raised almost £3000. I was overwhelmed by the support, from my family and friends and from people I'd never met, all sharing a common goal to end abuse towards women and children. No woman or child should live in fear, that was my mission to keep me motivated when parts of my walk would inevitably get tough.

"Ind, you'll be fine, I'll make sure of it. But you have to rest and get better properly. You can't ignore this otherwise you really won't be able to finish. You must allow your body to heal, ok?"
I snivel and reluctantly say "Ok..."

And just like that I'm torn away from my beloved path for two days. It's like a physical ache in my heart, a strange mourning, a deep yearning to be amongst the wilderness again. To be safe in her womb of unsafety. A peculiar paradox. I even miss sleeping on hard ground in my little tent, my vac-pac ration pouches, the strangely comforting burden of the weight of my backpack.

Dad spoke to his friend who is a physio and I'd developed what is called peroneal tendonitis, or lateral foot pain, which is a common injury among runners and long distance hikers. I spend the next two days lying down as much as possible, with my foot elevated and an ice pack strapped to it. Dad, bless him, in classic fashion, feeds me with everything but the kitchen sink and micromanages me with a strict regime of gentle exercises and the RICE treatment: Rest, Ice, Compression, Elevation.

All the while, I'm trying to stay positive. I will get back to my path, I think to myself. This is not the end. She and I have a whole lot of unfinished business. 450 miles of it to be exact. I honour and acknowledge little feelings of doubt and failure that start to creep in. It's a natural part of the process. I greet them warmly, I feel them, I see them, and then I let those feelings go on their way. I keep healing crystals of red jasper and rose quartz near at all times and do healing meditations before bed. I will heal. I will continue. I will finish this thing.

Day 18 and I ease myself back into my journey with a 13 mile flat local walk from Brixham to Babbacombe via Torquay in my home area of South Devon. I'm not supposed to reach this section for another few weeks yet, but I figure if I do it now, an easy section, now I've healed a lot from my injury, then when I reach this point in a few week's time I can go back to Hartland Quay and do the six mile section to Morwenstow I skipped. A bit higgledy-piggledy but at least I'll not have skipped any bits then, even if I did them in a topsy-turvy way.

The urban walk today is one I know like the back of my hand. A bit boring if I'm honest, the town of Torquay looking a bit sad, a forgotten relic of its 1950s English Riviera heyday. But it was a good one to get me back into it. I felt like I did at the very start of my walk, gingerly taking those steps like a newborn deer again. A little stiff to begin with but then loosened up ok.

But even so, I cried with happiness to be back with my beloved path again. Those acorn emblazoned wooden signposts had become my guiding light, my home these past few weeks and as I breathed in the fresh sea air, my eyes drinking in the expanse of the ocean before me, I thought "Yes. Honey, I'm home! I can do this."

Day 19 - back to Bedruthan steps to begin again where I left off. Oh, I was so excited to be properly back, I had butterflies in my stomach, my heart leapt with joy and relief.

I took it slow and steady for the six mile walk to Newquay, my foot feeling delicate but manageable, and it was a beautiful day. Windy but sunny, super refreshing and I revelled in the views of the choppy waves dancing about in the sunlight. White curls of sea foam can-canning around as if applauding my return.

Walking into Watergate Bay, melancholy began to wash over me... memories of long ago ebbed and flowed in my mind that a few weeks ago would've felt like a dagger to my heart, but now had the cloudy, diffused soft edges of sea glass.

One memory in particular stood out in the haze... a young couple tangled in an unhealthy attachment... their story is tarnished by pain...

Embracing in the swirling winds above Fruitful Cove, she searches his eyes for the light that was once bright, but is now fading like a candle running out of wax to burn. A tiny dingy boat in the middle of a raging storm. Where is the lighthouse? Where is the way forward?

I love you.

I love you too.

Does she?

I've written and rewritten this part of the book so many times. Wondering what and how much to say. Because whatever I say is going to impact the other person involved and the people around him. I've agonised about whether I should say anything at all. Time and time again we hear about women sharing their stories, only to be accused of overreacting or even lying. I've even thought to myself sometimes - what if I AM overreacting? But the hurt in my body ran deep and raw. And it was very much real.

I've chosen not to state his name, purely out of respect for a fellow human being, and to keep his anonymity. But I've also felt all the emotions about him along my healing journey. Pain: why did he have to hurt me so deeply? Anger: if he wanted a better story he should've treated me better. Guilt: what if I've made all his problems worse by leaving him? Grief: why couldn't he be the man I wanted him to be? And finally, Acceptance: whichever way you look at it, the eight years we spent together are part of both of us. This is as much my story to tell as it is his. And I truly believe it's an important story to tell. I genuinely wish him well in his life now. I hope he is happy. I hope he is healthy. I hope he leads a good life. I really do want that for him. Wherever he is now. Whoever he is now. Truly.

Time, along with a lot of inner work on myself, really does heal all wounds and I see our relationship now as a lesson my soul had to go through in order to become my highest self. But so many women suffer in relationships like this. And if my story helps one of them break free then it's worth it. So here it is.

Two months before my 20th birthday I fell in love for the first time. I met him at our local small-town pub and was instantly attracted to him. There was a deep darkness, an intensity in him that drew me in, although back then I wasn't sure why as he was cute but not physically my type. He bought me a jäger bomb, we danced the night away to reggae and then he walked me home and we passionately kissed in the doorway.

From that night on we became inseparable. We fell in love with the all-consuming, tunnel-vision nature of being in love for the first time. He was intense, attentive and always there. But there was something that was bubbling beneath the surface that I now know looking back felt uneasy about him. I noticed that uneasiness from the very first night we met. But I ignored my intuition as a young woman in the throes of first time passion and brushed it off as just what it must be like according to what I'd seen in the great love stories of my generation (Twilight, Sex & The City, Bridget Jones I'm looking at you here). And looking back now, there were red flags from the beginning warning me that the man I'd fallen for was troubled. Subtle things like jealousy, possessiveness, putting me on a pedestal, making me feel like a perfect little doll and not truly seeing me as a real, imperfect human. These things I thought were desirable at the time, and I now know that it massaged my inner ego and shadow wounds around being virginal, saintly, innocent, a saviour so I could go to my childhood upbringing's version of "heaven". But in reality, were dangerous signs of things to come.

A couple of years into our relationship we moved in together and that's when the problems started. The man I fell in love with started to disappear and in his place was revealed the deeply, deeply troubled person he truly was. Maybe the man I fell in love with was only ever his potential self, a mirage and not the real him.

He started to become consumed by the darkness within himself. He never physically hit me, but I always did everything I could to keep his demons from verbally lashing out at me. The threat, the fear I felt was always there. He would sit in the dark staring into space for hours and would push me away every time I asked what was wrong. Would only speak to me to criticise and barely spent time with me. Would rather go to bed immediately after I'd cook him dinner than spend quality time with me. Would tell me to shut up and be quiet if I so much as started humming a song. If I so much as showed an ounce of joy. I always had to ask permission if I wanted to invite my family or a friend round to our house and even if I did ask for permission he would get annoyed.

Communicating with him was like trying to draw blood from a stone. And that's what he became. A cold stone. When I looked into his eyes it just looked... like a black hole. With a darkness that frightened me.

He was diagnosed with clinical depression and anxiety and referred to a counsellor for a three month period of CBT therapy. But after those three months, the system, so underfunded by the government, dropped him like a piece of trash. I felt so desperately sad and helpless, I loved him, but I just couldn't understand why this love wasn't being reciprocated. How could the man I'd fallen for be suffering like this with the cosy, loving life we'd built together? Where did he go? Who was this person so dead inside?

He opened up to me a little about past traumas and I had hope that he could get better.

But things only seemed to get worse in the following six years. I constantly had to ask for affection, ask to be loved. I was giving everything I had, my body, my heart, my soul to him and he wasn't giving anything but toxicity back to me. There are parts of our relationship that will always be too private to share in this book but I will say our relationship became very toxic and co-dependant.

I found myself living my life dictated by another person and their mood swings. Everyday I dedicated myself to making his life better, cooking him delicious healthy meals (which he'd turn his nose up at like a petulant child), trying to plan activities (which he never had the enthusiasm to do), giving my body to him when I didn't want to. I poured myself into researching depression & anxiety and how I can be the most supportive and loving partner to someone with these issues.

But he made me feel terrified that if I ever left him he would kill himself... and yet no matter what I did for him, he would constantly mope around the house saying he hated his life and was going to kill himself anyway.

When we had sex it was no longer passionate for me. It was rough, painful and I faked orgasms every time because I was so fearful about making his mental health worse. Biting into a pillow from the pain, face down to hide my tears, I performed in the way he wanted me to. He told me if I did these sexual things for him it would make him feel better. And I lied to him and told him I enjoyed all the things he wanted me to do when in reality it sickened me to my core and filled me with the deepest dread. I lied to myself as well and convinced myself that maybe I just wasn't a sexual person, maybe I couldn't have orgasms or experience pleasure?

I felt scared, always on edge, desperately sad but numb at the same time and so confused as to what I was doing wrong. Aren't I enough? Why does he hate the life we'd created together so much? What more can I do to make him better? On and on this internal anguish continued. Constantly overthinking everything I said and did. Carefully planning every word, every action, for fear of being responsible for someone's sadness. My mind was like a dense, dark, lonely forest, thick with twisting brambles and knife-like thorns that punctured my heart. I couldn't find my way out of it.

I'd discreetly spend hours late at night, or early in the morning, scouring the internet, searching for help from mental health charities. So many mental health websites say that, as a partner of someone with depression, you shouldn't push them to open up, you should be gentle and patient and live life on their terms and in other words tread on eggshells around them constantly. Of course, I'm not trying to be disrespectful of the wonderful work that mental health charities do as I know that they can be a life saving resource, and of course I'm not a professional psychiatrist myself, but frankly, in my opinion, the advice they give to loved ones is often very damaging and counter-productive.

No one should have to give up their life, their own well-being for someone else. It doesn't matter how messed up your husband, wife or partner is, if they are treating you badly, you have every right to walk away. This shouldn't be controversial to say, but do NOT give up your birthright to happiness for someone with mental illness if they are not willing to do the inner work on themselves. It's not your job. They are NOT your responsibility. Read that again: they are NOT your responsibility. Trust me, I've been there.

Sometimes there would be glimmers of hope when I tried to tell him how I felt and how his behaviour was affecting me. He would desperately beg me not to leave him, tell me he wouldn't be able to live without me and promise to change, and he would for a few weeks. And I would always be the one to end up apologising for being "crazy" and "irrational". But then he would slip back into his old ways and didn't seem to have any motivation to truly change. If I tried to flag up his behaviour he would gaslight me and say "you'll get over it." I was trapped in a vicious cycle of servitude to a man I no longer loved but felt terrified to leave in case of what would happen if I did. How could I live with myself if someone ended their own life because of me?

But I wasn't totally the victim in this situation. Of course, nothing that happened was ever my fault... But it was MY responsibility to take action and change what was hurting me in MY life. But I didn't. For eight years. I was lying to both of us by pretending that everything was ok and that I still loved him. What I've learnt since is that there was a subconscious part of me, my inner child that grew up in a controlling religion, that relished being the martyr, the saviour, the giver, the victim. I catered to him and pandered to him and when that dedication wasn't reciprocated, my ego subconsciously enjoyed saying "poor me" and "this is just what I have to do to get into heaven".

I confided in my Mum and my best friend Betsy. He had sworn me to secrecy about what was going on, saying that no one would care but I couldn't live like that. I had to speak to someone. The two most important women in my life urged me to be careful and think hard about what I wanted in life. They respected my decision to stick by him but I could tell they wanted me out of that situation.

The year 2020 rolled around and that year changed everything. It changed everything for every single person on this planet. The COVID-19 pandemic put life into perspective for everyone and I was no exception. I slowly and painfully fell out of love with him. The national lockdowns intensified the emotional abuse I was suffering at home. There was no escape. I would silently cry myself to sleep beside him every night, wondering when I would ever get out. Christmas Eve came around and that really was a turning point.

Betsy had invited me to a small gathering at her house and I was really excited to go. To be myself and forget about everything for one night. He didn't want me to go, of course. He never wanted me to do anything with the only friend I had left but I finally stood up to him and told him I was going. It didn't go down well and I was ordered to be back by midnight. It was such a lovely evening, I had a couple drinks, lots of great conversation and some lighthearted flirting. I hadn't felt that at ease since..... well since my late teens. But the closer it drew to midnight, the closer I became on edge. I was like bloody Cinderella. I got home at quarter past midnight and that pretty much ruined Christmas. The following few days felt worse than treading on eggshells. I was treading on a thousand wasp nests praying not to be stung.

A few days later, I met up with Betsy. I needed help. I couldn't take it anymore. I was becoming a hollow husk of myself, I didn't love him anymore, I didn't want to waste my life with a man who was completely and utterly emotionally unavailable. That's when she said something that I will never forget. Something that I had known in my heart to be true for years, but didn't have the strength to take action on it before.

"India. I'm only going to say this once: I want you to leave him. Please. You deserve so much better. Enough now." my soul-sister said, with tears in her eyes.

My very being shattered. My heart cracked open with all the pain and molten lava of a volcano erupting. My spiritual awakening had begun.

I couldn't argue with her, she was right. I had to get out before I completely disappeared, or worse, if children came along. I couldn't bring children up in that environment. We cried in each other's arms on her teal velvet sofa. She cradled my head like a small child as I sobbed into the crook of her warm elbow. My hot salty tears soaking her jumper. We made an escape plan, and on Saturday the 2nd of January 2021 I finally left him.

It was the scariest, most painful, most traumatic day of my life. I'd never experienced heartbreak before, I was riddled with guilt and couldn't get his face out of my head when I told him I was leaving him. He looked panic-stricken, as pale as snow. I kept a few metres distance from him as I finally uncaged my truth in a whirlwind of tears and words that had been trapped inside for so long. He looked erratic and volatile and I lingered by the front door of our house so I could make a swift exit if it came to that. I knew my decision was the right thing to do, for both of us, but I couldn't help but fear for his life. And in that moment, mine.

I reach Quarryfields campsite on the other side of the River Gannel past Fistral Beach on day 19 of my SWCP adventure and spend the rest of the day gently massaging and resting my feet. I feel exhausted emotionally and physically, a little foggy mentally which I had kind of been anticipating when I thought about walking through Newquay with all the memories popping up. But still so thankful to be on this path, thankful that I'd gotten this town out of the way. Clear head for tomorrow, I thought. You're approaching the depths of Cornwall now. My stomach flipped at the thought, my mind conjuring up Alice tumbling down her rabbit hole. I'm ready.

I woke at my usual time of 7:30am on the morning of my twentieth day to the smell of the most delicious air I think I've ever breathed. The rising buttercup-yellow sun was gently enveloping her Earth as if cradling a sleeping baby, fluffy candy floss clouds rolled across the pale blue sky and a brisk wind whispered hints of a northern storm.

I rejoined the coast path at Crantock Beach after a hard night's sleep at the campsite, my grogginess quickly whipped away by the breeze and the stunning views of turquoise seas and pale sandy beaches. From there it was a tiring but satisfying ramble around the West Pentire peninsula, an exhausting trudge through Holywell sand dunes and around the eerie military training grounds of Penhale Point. It looked like something out of an apocalypse movie complete with burnt out houses and empty corrugated iron bunkers.

After that came a sight that sent my spirits soaring in awe: the massive three mile expanse of Perranporth beach. I excitedly scrambled down the cliff side, tore off my sweaty walking boots and socks, strapped them to the outside of my pack, rolled up my leggings and hobbled over to the water's edge. My left foot was starting to ache again and as I stepped into the ice cold salt water, I swear I could physically hear the hiss coming from my burning feet like when you plunge a hot frying pan into the washing up bowl.

"Ahhhhhh, this feels soooo GOOOOOOD!!" I exclaimed into the wind. I walked the entire three mile length of Perranporth beach barefoot through the briskly crashing waves. Although it was a struggle walking through the wet sand and waves with the weight of my pack sinking me down and feeling like I was taking one step forward and two steps back, the reward of the cold healing water soothing my bottom half made it so worth it. The sand provided a gentle exfoliation of the now cured-leather-hard soles of my feet, the salt water a calming ointment for my tired muscles.

Before I started my walk, I'd had romantic notions about how everyday, after I would finish a day's walking, I'd do some yoga on the beach and then go for a swim afterwards as the sun was setting. But the reality was that I was so tired at the end of each day, it was all I could do to crawl into my tent, shove some food into my growling stomach, lie down and try to sleep. It was also true that for most of the walk so far, the sea hadn't even been accessible for all the towering cliffs and rocky headland. So to finally wade through the sea this afternoon was bliss, even if it was just a paddle.

By the time I reached Perranporth Touring Campsite, I was once again knackered and very wobbly on the hard tarmac road after the length of soft sand-walking. I staggered into the campsite entrance as a family of four were walking out. They whooped and cheered and shouted "You must be hiking the coast path! You

made it to the next stop! You look exhausted!
Well done!"
"Haha yes I am... aww thank you!" I replied, tears
in my eyes, surprised and a little overwhelmed
by the welcoming party. Wow I really must look
worn out, I thought.

I chose a spot after checking in with the lovely
lady in her 60s who ran the place and my pack
and I collapsed in a heap in a sheltered spot
beneath a line of trees. I heard sympathetic
giggles and whispers of "aww look at her, bless
her, she's exhausted." coming from my fellow
campers behind me, but I was too tired to turn
around and acknowledge them.

I'd just managed to quickly put up my tent
before the heavy rain that I'd smelled that
morning arrived.
"Cold rations again for dinner then." I said to
myself. Moroccan style bean stew the label on
the vac-pac stated, but my taste buds barely had
a chance to taste it, I gobbled it down that
quickly. My stomach grumbled impatiently as I
drifted off to sleep that night, but my heart and
soul felt fulfilled.

Day 21, wake up, protein shake, go to the loo,
pack stuff away, set off. My new everyday
morning routine is becoming second nature to
me now. I climbed up into the cliffs above
Porthtowan to what felt like another planet.
Strange terrain with unusual black, red and

white rock formations dominated the landscape. The path undulated and swept around these rock formations like an off-road rally race track. Stranger still were the spooky old abandoned tin mine buildings dotted about here and there. Standing with the solemn pride of a forgotten industrial heritage, the backdrop of heavy darkening clouds made these buildings look even more dramatic and post-apocalyptic.

Approaching the picturesque little town of St Agnes, the path began to get busy with holidaymakers and it's easy to see why as it's every bit the quintessential Cornish seaside town. But I hurried past - the Cornwall that had my heart in its grasp was beyond. Up there, amongst the gorse, bracken and rock. Amongst the birds, the butterflies and grass snakes, that's where I was meant to be. I'd completely surrendered to the wilderness, body and soul, and it was a stunningly bracing cliff top hike around St Agnes Head, above Tubby's Head and finally finishing at Porthtowan.

Along my journey so far, even the excruciating first couple weeks, I'd felt such a deep and utter happiness with where my life was going and where it was at that moment. But behind that deep happiness was a curious sense of grief that rose to the surface every now and again. As I rambled across the cliff tops to Porthtowan, my heart got pulled in two directions. I was so so happy, yet grief quietly came to say hello as well.

I mused for a while about this, my steps falling into a steady rhythm, allowing my mind to roam free. I think, when you experience true happiness, the paradox of grief is naturally the other side of the coin that comes with it. For it's only when you've been through trauma and sadness in your life, that happiness becomes all the more meaningful and important. And it meant everything to me that I was following my true soul path, here and now, finally.

Staggering into Porthtowan after a solid 10 mile hike, I was ready to stop for the day. There was just one more massive hill to climb before I got to my next campsite. There was always one more massive hill! I began the slow ascent, pausing often for a breather and my usual motivational speeches - "C'mon India, one more hill! One... more... hill!"

At last, I walked into Porthtowan Touring Park, a little generic looking, but a safe spot to camp for the night.
"You can't camp here tonight. We're full. Covid." said the snooty lady behind the till at reception.
"Oh no, really?! But.. but I only need a small patch of grass... I can see plenty of spaces I could go to?"
"No you can't, because of Covid we have to stick to the numbers. Sorry." she wasn't sorry in the slightest.

"Oh please, I'm hiking the coast path for charity, it's the end of the day and I'm exhausted, is there really nowhere I could pitch my tiny one person tent? I'm happy to pay a pitch fee." tears were prickling in my eyes now.

"Sorry. That's just the rules. There's another campsite about a mile away. You could try there." she said monotonously, bored with my presence.

"Oh... Ok then... Well, thanks." I turned around and walked out onto the driveway, helplessly looking at my map for somewhere else to camp.

All the while this sorry scene was playing out, a Tesco delivery driver had pulled into the campsite to deliver a large grocery shop to one of the caravans.

"Do you need a lift, love? There's Mount Pleasant Eco Park five mins drive away." Tesco-man said. He had a lovely, kind, round face with a matching round belly.

"Oh yes please thank you so much! As long as it isn't too much out of your delivery route?"

"Not at all, love! I'm passing by there now if you want to jump in?"

And so I jumped in gladly, feeling relieved that I didn't have to find my own way to this mysterious sounding place.

Tesco-man dropped me at Mount Pleasant Eco Park as promised, five mins later.

"Do you have enough food for tonight, love? You must be starving, you look like you could do with some more meat on your bones! Here, take these crisps and a choccy bar, you need them more than I do!" he said, chuckling as he patted his belly.

"Aww thank you, honestly thank you so much, your kindness means so much to me." I replied, sincerely.

"Don't mention it, I'm glad to help a young lady in distress. I couldn't believe that receptionist turned you away, I couldn't just leave you stranded there!"

I waved off my lovely delivery-man, faith in humanity restored, and wandered into my new end-point for the evening. And wow! I was actually glad that first campsite turned me away, because what I had just walked into was so much more up my alley! Mount Pleasant Ecological Park is an eco community and quirky wild-campsite a couple miles inland from the coast path nestled amongst the vast expanse of farmland that blankets this area. Walking through it was like walking through a festival; there was a communal kitchen with a barbeque and dining area, a communal shower block and toilets area that was powered by solar and an open teepee tent draped with fairy lights with a guy playing a guitar to a chilled out audience of dreadlocks and harem trousers. My kind of place indeed.

I walked up to the wooden shack reception and was greeted by the lovely hippie girl that managed the small camping field. We bonded over the fact that we had the same walking sandals - turquoise strappy rubber things from, of course, Mountain Warehouse. She welcomed me with open arms and showed me to a lovely soft grassy area behind a lush bramble hedge that had beautiful views overlooking the farmland and then the ocean beyond, which seemed very far away in the distance.

"Well, this worked out so much better than that other boring vanilla campsite!" I said to myself settling in to watch the sun set on a very satisfying day. I'd just got back to my tent after watching guitar-guy for a while, followed by a surprisingly luxurious solar-powered shower and quickly began to fall asleep, starting to feel very settled into the routine of the wilderness. Everyday was bringing something magical. I couldn't wait to see what tomorrow brought.

Week 4 – Clean Slate

Day 22 and I woke to a steady stream of rain falling on my little shelter and the delicious smell of the land being cleansed. It's hard to describe - that elusive yet addictive smell of rain. Sweet and musky, but with a tang of something sour. I breathed slowly & deeply and drank it in as I began my morning routine. Protein shake, go to the loo, brush teeth, pack away everything, let's go.

"Wooooaaahahhaha! Oh gosh, careful, carefu- woooopsy!"

Swirling wind and rain was throwing me around like a ragdoll today. The path itself wasn't too strenuous, but the weather made it quite tiring as the ground became a slush of slippery gravel. I giggled as I kept slipping over into the sodden gorse bushes. Thankfully there weren't as many sheer cliff faces today that I could've flown off, but there were strange pillows of water-saturated grass patches that, when I jumped up and down on them, sloshed around like a water balloon. It was a simple but unusual thing that had me laughing and gasping in wonder like a child. There was no one around today, just me, the elements and the world at my feet.

A little way along the path out of Porthtowan, I saw the first and only person I'd see on the trail that day, coming quickly up behind me.

"You must be as crazy as I am!" I yelled cheerfully to the man into the howling wind. He was young, in his early twenties, with a big bushy beard, strong legs and kitted out in gear that I recognised. A fellow long distance hiker, of course, for who else would be out walking on a day like today?

"Haha yeah, we are the crazy ones, for sure! I'm hiking the coast path for a week just to get away for a bit. How much are you doing?" he said.

"The whole thing! You're the first person I've seen today, and probably the only! You go first, you'll be quicker than I am."

"Ah you're the first and only person I've seen today too! Wow, well done you, enjoy and stay safe, yeah? See you down the path!" and off he went, positively galloping along, he was out of sight before I knew it.

"Wooooopsy!"
"... ohhhhh-woopsy-woah there!"
"Woah woah woah... oof!"

The winds kept whipping, the rain kept lashing, it was so strong that I could put all my weight against it, lean face forward and not fall. It was a battle to push through as I hiked along the craggy cliff top farmland to Portreath. It was late morning, I was soaked through to my bones, cold yet sweaty at the same time and absolutely

craving pastry and a warm cup of something. The Portreath Bakery was the flame to my moth, the beacon of light that I ran towards like a starving vulture. The lovely owner welcomed me in and the smell of warm baked goods almost sent me spiralling into a werewolf-like stupor. "Oooh, a hot chocolate please! Oh and a large steak pasty... ooh ooh and that big danish pastry there as well please." I said greedily, my eyes wide, my mouth salivating.
"Haha, oh my goodness, you look like you need this, my lovely! Here you go, enjoy, have a sit down and warm yourself up." she said.

Ecstasy. Pure ecstasy. That's the only word for it. Frothy cocoa, joy in liquid form, slipping down my throat like honey. Savoury, buttery pastry enveloped tender pieces of meat and potatoes suspended in a silky gravy-embrace. Then, cinnamon, icing sugar and feathery-cushiony-softy-doughy-gloriousness. My lips savoured every bite, it took all my willpower to take my time and not devour my early lunch all in one bite. It was amazing. I was completely lost in the moment of eating. A few people passed by giving me amused looks as if I was an alien visiting this beautiful planet for the first time. I would have given funny looks too - here was a sodden, smelly wild-woman dressed head-to-toe in varying forms of waterproof Gore-Tex, hood gathered around her head making her look like ET, massive pack half the size of her on her back, groaning in complete rapture at eating a humble Cornish Pasty.

Feeling warm, full and satisfied, I pushed on once more through the wind and rain out of Portreath and up into the wild cliff tops. My pastry-fest had given me a boost of energy as I strode through the stormy atmosphere with vigour and determination. The clouds were dark, the air was thick with moisture and the ground swelled, pregnant with the fresh fertilisation falling from the sky. Back bent forward at a 45 degree angle, arms swinging like pendulums holding the poles, legs rhythmically keeping pace, and my face squinting and grinning maniacally as it got sprayed like a windscreen down a motorway, I was in my element, literally. But then-

"wooOP-AGH!"

Mother Earth swept me up in a strong gust of air, everything went slow motion in the opposite direction, my feet were flailing towards the dark grey sky, the rough, rumbling ocean was suddenly above me, not below me, and my body went hurtling down into a tangle of heather and gorse. My heart leapt into my throat.

"Oh god oh god oh god. Where am I? Are you ok, India? Hurt? Let's see. Feet feel ok. Ankles feel ok. Head feels ok. Back feels ok. Hips... ooh ouch..." I said to myself. The spikes of the gorse had penetrated my hips and backside through my waterproofs and I could feel scratches and rashes already forming. I looked around and realised I'd fallen left in an inland direction, thankfully, and not down the sheer cliff face to my right. Panic reverberated through my body as it dawned on me how close I'd come to a much worse situation. The adrenaline, the momentum suddenly drained from my body. Once again my beloved path had humbled me. I was knackered. Time to stop for the day.

Late afternoon, I staggered into the cute little village of Gwithian just as the rain was finally beginning to ease and was welcomed warmly into Gwithian Farm Campsite by the promise of a pizza van coming later that evening. I nestled my tent amongst the palm trees and pampas grasses and skipped off to the bathroom for the most blissful hot shower. The warm water heated my salt-cured skin and soothed the rashes on my bum from my fall earlier.

Pizza time!
"Phooaaaarr", I swooned over the stone-baked crust, the bbq jackfruit topping with rich tomato sauce, fresh basil and vegan mozzarella. Food had become one of the highlights of my days. I'd never appreciated it so much in my life as I sat crouched in my tent with the cardboard box across my lap, the waves of delicious aroma filling my little shelter with sweet savoury delight.

I fell asleep quickly and deeply as soon as my head hit my little navy blow up pillow, with a full belly as I snuggled, fully clothed as usual, into my sleeping bag. I'd completed three weeks on the SWCP. My life had changed, I had changed. I relished the thought of having such a long way to go still. Yes. This is the life.

Day 23 and I woke up in a mini version of The Caribbean. Green palm trees arced their way over my tent against a backdrop of the most vibrant blue sky I've ever seen. The air was hot with salt, sun and surf. I eagerly packed up and got going at 7:30am.

From Gwithian, the path undulated and ambled for three miles through the Upton Towans nature reserve. A stretch of beautiful sand dunes decorated with an abundance of hardy green and yellow grasses and wildlife, it was a breathtaking sight with the large triangular slate waymarkers guiding my way. The sandy terrain was a little tough to trudge through, but the views of the massive expanse of the golden beach and blue sea beyond rewarded my efforts tenfold. Along the way I breathed loud and contented sighs of happiness, stretching my arms wide, revelling in the wide open spaces.

Eventually, I strolled into Hayle and was met by a massive construction sight. I felt more than a little jarred at being surrounded by such loud industry and machinery, "surely the path doesn't go through THIS? This is horrid! And boring!" I mused to myself. Loud diggers angrily busting up concrete, massive cranes swinging poles of steel around in a robotic jousting match, wire fences, the smell of pollution, tired agitated workers in high-vis and slowly rising up out of it all were the foundations of expensive holiday apartments and second homes.

"Little boxes, on the hillside, little boxes made of ticky-tacky, little boxes, little boxes and they all look just the same..." I hummed that famous tune to myself. There was no other way but to go through it.

I kept referring to my map to check that I was going the right way, the coast path signs seemed to have completely disappeared and the loud concrete jungle was a maze to navigate through. I felt wholly out of place and a little panicky to be away from my haven of natural wilderness. Two miles later the penny dropped.

Shit.
I'd been going in totally the opposite direction. "How is this possible?!" I yelled into the white noise of steel and concrete. In the wild, I've never once been lost. But as soon as I get into civilization my sense of direction completely goes out the window!

"FUCK! So that's four miles I've wasted today... uuuuggghhhh!!"

I plodded back the way I came to try and find the coast path again. It was tedious and my body was growing tired from the heat and walking on hard concrete. I stuck out my thumb. "Urgggh I just want to get to St Ives now!" I grumbled to myself, resenting wasting four miles total going the wrong way.

Only a minute later and a black taxi cab pulled up beside me. A lovely man in his 50s with short silver fluffy hair greeted me from the window. "Ooh would it be possible to hitch a lift into St Ives? Only, I'm hiking the coast path but I've been going the wrong way and had hoped to push on to Zennor and I'm meeting my Dad for a resupply you see... urm... but now I'm getting quite tired and... and..." a curious lump formed in my throat then as I rambled on.
"Oh of course! I'm not sure I'm technically allowed to pick up hitchhikers but I'm going into St Ives anyway. Come on in, that's fine." he said with a kind smile.

I chatted the usual conversation to the taxi driver about what I was doing and why, where I was headed etc. It crossed my mind that perhaps I would get bored of having the same conversation with different people everyday, but it didn't get boring at all. Everyone I'd met on this path so far had been so kind and helpful to me, and they'd all had their own fascinating story to tell as well.

People are good. I know this to be absolutely true. The bad things in this world are only born out of feelings of fear and anger that people do not know how to deal with. I know this to be absolutely true as well. If everyone did inner work on themselves or took themselves off on an adventure or just did something, anything, that enables them to look inward, I know that humanity will heal.

It was a five minute ride into St Ives and the taxi driver insisted I not pay for my ride.
"Oh no I want to! Honestly, here take this £5 at least." I said.
"No no, love. I was coming this way anyway so it doesn't matter."
"No honestly, take it, at least as a tip, haha!"
"Oh alright, go on then, thank you. I'm just happy to help!"

St Ives was as expected: a throng of crowded streets, dropped ice creams and greedy seagulls ready to dive-bomb their next victim. I enjoy visiting St Ives, but today I couldn't wait to get away from civilization once more and immerse myself in my beloved wild. The path climbed steeply up into the cliffs and soon became almost untraceable amongst the bog patches, streams and boulders that dominated this next section.

In the SWCP guidebook, this section was supposedly severe due to its remoteness, but I was loving it. One could easily lose their way in this terrain. There wasn't really a path at all in some sections. But here, amongst my queendom, I knew I could never get lost. The boulders I had to scramble over were my friends, nestled amongst the bracken and gorse like plump forest trolls, with various funky lichen-hairstyles.

I'd had a sudden surge in energy since leaving the urban suffocation of Hayle & St Ives. I clambered over the tricky terrain with somewhat ease, helped along by my poles adding valuable stability, and skipped over the streams of clear water. Oh, the water looked so tempting, I couldn't resist stopping at various points to splash my hot face and neck with the crystal clear liquid bliss. I reached for my drinking water. The day was getting really hot now and I'd worked up a proper sweat yomping up and down the rollercoaster path for the past five miles.

Oh god... oh this is not good. I only had a thumb's worth of water left in my water bottle. My 10l water bag in my pack was empty. "Ohhhhh shit India... we've still got three miles to go until Zennor! There's nowhere for water until then!... ok ok ok we'll be fine... just take tiny sips, it'll be fine" I tried to tell myself.

Throughout my journey so far, I hadn't needed to fill up more than two litres of water at a time. The SWCP is so well connected that one is never that far away from a source of clean drinking water. But today was the first day when I actually felt scared that I wouldn't have enough.

The next three miles seemed to stretch on endlessly. I tried to go as fast as I could so I could get to Zennor for water quicker, but then I would sweat more and lose more water and risk dehydration. The boulders were no longer my friends. It made the hiking incredibly slow going as I picked my way through like a toddler just learning to walk. The sun beat down in a relentless torture, baking the little bucket hat on my head which had now crystallized from the salted remains of my sweat.

The path was lonely. It was just me and her. And a battle with my mind to keep going. I kept checking my map to try and guess how far away I was from Zennor. The landscape made it impossible to gauge. Rock after gorse bush after rock after bracken after rock. On and on and on. Through the brisk hot salt wind, I pushed on, losing my footing a couple times as my body started to beg for us to stop for the day.

"Not yet... There's no water... nowhere to camp... not yet... we have to keep going... come on India... you can fucking do it..."

Dad was meeting me at Zennor for a resupply which greatly helped to spur me on those last few miles and, at last, the path took a turning inland to the village centre. I reached the village car park next to the thatched roof pub and found Tilly, my little black Toyota Aygo that Dad was borrowing for the duration of my trip, baking in the late afternoon sun. I plonked myself down beside her in the tiny square of shade she cast on the dusty gravel ground and leant my sweat soaked back against her thick tyres. It was so good to see her, my little car that never failed me, was a strange oasis-like reminder of my life in the normal world.

Dad was nowhere to be seen. "Hmm, odd... he might be in the pub..." I muttered to myself. I thought about getting up and going to look for him but quickly decided that I couldn't be bothered. I was hot, sweaty, thirsty and tired and decided that I'll just wait with Tilly until he comes along. I realised I'd done my longest walk so far - 15 miles in one day! Setting off from Gwithian this morning seemed like a distant memory. I was so proud of myself. Exhausted but completely fulfilled.

"There you are, Indy-pops!" Dad came strolling in from the direction of the coast path I'd just walked along 10 minutes before. He saw me panting in my tiny patch of shade, propped up against Tilly, legs stretched out in front of me, and immediately started fussing, feeding and watering me with tuna-cucumber-saladcream sandwiches, chocolate Penguin bars and salt & vinegar crisps.

"I was waiting on the hill over there, looking out for you with my binoculars! You must've come up so quickly I missed you! Are you alright, my treasure?"

"Hey, Dad. I'm ok, I'm so thirsty, I ran out of water three miles ago, I'm ok though don't worry. I walked 15 miles today!" I said trying to seem like I had more energy than I really had.

"Oh Ind, well done! You've done so well, my love, I'm so proud of you. This section's really remote, huh? I've done some exploring for you again. There's literally nowhere to camp. You can't camp on the path because it's all gorse and rock and cliff faces. And besides that it's just private farmland. The next campsite is Trevaylor Campsite, about six or seven miles down the line at Botallack, let's just go there today, hey? Don't bother with these next six miles my love. It's so remote, there'll be no facilities and nowhere for water and no flat surface to camp on and-and-"

"Ok, ok Dad, it's ok. Let's go to Trevaylor. I don't mind skipping this bit." I said, cutting off his worried ramble.

And I really didn't mind skipping this next section around Pendeen. Up until now, I didn't want to skip sections and I grappled with feelings of guilt about not being a purist thru-hiker. But I had to listen to my body. I had to be smart around surviving in the wild. Time and time again, this path had humbled me and brought me to my knees with my mortal physical limits.

And yet. I'd completely fallen in love with her. My path. My coast path. Every day she turned my soul inside-out and enabled me to discover things about myself that I didn't know were there. Or maybe I had just forgotten they were there.

I set up camp at Botallack, said my goodbyes to my amazing Dad, I could tell he was breathing a sigh of relief that I wasn't wild-camping, and settled in for the evening. Beans and veggie sausage on the camping stove again and a giant Cherry Bakewell tart that Dad had brought, I took my time savouring every bite.

The sun began to set behind some exquisite cloud formations tonight. Wispy, fluffy trails of pink, red and yellow candy floss floated through the sky like jellyfish tendrils. The bright blue daytime sky now turned muted shades of cornflower and violet and I became drowsy in my sleeping bag looking at it. Tomorrow I will reach the tip of the British Isles and begin the long journey along the southern side of the SWCP. I am ready.

Day 24. I set off from Botallack, rejoined the coast path and was greeted by fascinating old mining buildings. Many abandoned stone tubular structures and fenced off mine shafts dotted the landscape and I felt somewhat melancholy looking at them. Lichen, grasses and creeping plants now grew abundantly on these relics that once were the home of a thriving, bustling industry, but now bore the scars of modernisation, globalisation and capitalism. But here they still stood, proud and watchful, strong in their presence, telling tales of old, reminding us all of our ancestors that paved the way for our luxuries of today.

The walking has been nothing short of spectacularly varied today and I wandered in awe the whole time, my eyes wide, my mouth agog at the sheer amount of things to look at. Leaving the mining buildings behind, I came to stone structures of a more rugged and wild kind. Jagged granite tors like the ones I was so used to seeing at home on Dartmoor, pierced through the Earth's crust like dragons creeping out of their dark chambers. Their spiky noses pointed towards the bright warm sunshine, vampiric as if seeing the golden glow for the first time, instantly turning to stone as the light touched their scaly skin.

The tip of the British Isles was reaching ever nearer and I was so fully present in my surroundings today. I was thriving. Receiving the abundance. And loving every second. A short way in the distance, I saw a fellow long distance hiker. Unmistakable with all the matching gear as me: large backpack, leggings, sports t-shirt, hiking boots, walking poles. I came up behind him and honestly fell in love a little bit.

His name is Harry, he is 74 years young, tall and in incredible shape for his age and was walking the SWCP for a week. But get this: he was hiking as a training exercise for an ultra-marathon. In Iceland. I was in awe. What an inspiration!

"Yes, I just love hiking and running. Keeps me young, I say! I truly think that is the way to live a long, healthy, happy life: keep moving. Don't stop, otherwise you'll turn stale as bread." he added after he'd told me his adventures and plans for the next year.
"Harry, you are just amazing! So inspiring, thank you for sharing that with me! What other things have you done? Do you do lots of marathons?" I asked my new friend.
"Oh yes, my dear, I've run the London Marathon 15 times."
"WHAT?! Wow! Oh that's just incredible!" it was all I could say, my mouth opening and closing like a goldfish.

Harry and I walked the next few miles together to Cape Cornwall, the stunningly rugged outpost that many locals herald as the true marker of Land's End, and not the tourist park that sat a few miles south. I struggled to keep up with him as we spurred each other on with the prospect of a hot cup of tea and use of a flushing loo at

the tiny cafe there, but were bitterly
disappointed when we got there and saw it was
closed.

Nevertheless, the landscape of this area was
something quite special. It really did feel like the
edge of the world. So remote with barren grassy
headlands swept and battered by the Atlantic
winds, rocky cliff faces that seemed to change
with every crash of messy waves and old stone
farmhouse buildings that looked as if they'd
been there since the beginning of time.

"Harry, I'm going to linger here a while and take
in the atmosphere. You go on ahead, I don't
want to slow you down!" I said as Harry and I
stood in front of the hill that led up to the iconic
Cape Cornwall chimney stack.
"Ok, India. Thank you for your companionship
today! I will see you at some point down the
path I'm sure." he replied. And with that, he went
charging on up the hill onto the cliff-tops again
with the vigour of someone half his age. Wow, I
thought to myself, he really is quite amazing.

I eased myself down on the stunted grass beside
the chimney stack and soaked in my
surroundings, resting my back against my pack,
not bothering to take the straps off my
shoulders. The salt wind brushed through my
hair and gave me love-bites on my blushing
cheeks. My eyes squinted into the bright light of
the day. Everything looked so crystal clear, the

atmosphere in this part of the world so clean and fresh. Sea-birds hovered on the coastal upcurrent, eyeing up their next catch of the day in the swirling salt water below.

My heart swelled in my chest as a wide smile of contentment spread across my face. This is my life. Here. Right now. On this path. Tears welled in my eyes from gratitude.

I carried on and the path continued its rugged amble. More rocky tors came and sometimes I had to rock-climb over them, shoving my poles under my arms and scrabbling on all fours like a gecko slithering through a crevice in a stone wall. All along the path today there was an abundance of a most peculiar plant. Succulent-like with juicy finger tendrils spilling everywhere, and decorated with stunning vibrant purple flowers. Hottentot Fig, also known as Ice Plant: it was everywhere. Growing from every crevice of rock, every grassy patch, and the closer I got to Sennen Cove, the more abundant it became amongst the sandy coves and dunes of that area.

I climbed the steep road out of Sennen Cove, pretty exhausted after the rollercoaster of 9 miles and the heat of the day, passed by a couple of farmers in a Landrover that chuckled at my plight, and eventually reached Seaview Campsite. The reception desk looked closed. Doors locked. Lights out. Hmm. I started to panic

a little. According to the map, this was the only
campsite for miles around. I was exhausted,
really hungry and in need of a cooling shower. I
knocked on the door and, to my relief, a woman
came and unlocked it.

"Oh hi there! I'm hiking the coast path and I
wondered if you might have space for me to
pitch my tent in for the evening?"
The woman gave me what could only be
described as the filthiest look plastered across
her face ever, scanning me up and down,
narrowed eyes, mouth formed in a twisted
grimace of disgust that she clearly had no
intention of hiding.
"We don't take hikers here." she said with
disdain.
"Oh really? But, but... I-I'm hiking for charity, I'm
raising money for Women's Aid you see, I'm
doing the entire SWCP in one go and... and I only
have a tiny one-man tent. Don't you have a tiny
patch of grass and some fresh water I could
have? I'll pay of course!" I said in my sweetest
pleading voice, giving my best puppy-dog eyes.
"No. Rules are rules. We don't take hikers."
"Oh... but you're the only campsite around! Could
I at least fill up my water bag?" What am I going
to do?! I thought.
"No. We don't have space for you. Simple as that.
We can't just let you pitch on some grass. It's
only for our caravanners to use. There is a
campsite about 50 metres down the road. But
it's just a field." she said wrinkling her nose with

disgust as she described this mystery off-map campsite.

"Hff.. Huh... Ok, then. Well thanks anyway, I guess." I said with more than a hint of sarcasm in my voice. I turned away from the reception door and slumped down on the low wall in front of it, making sure I made a big show of looking all forlorn and tired so they'd feel guilty.

I couldn't believe how they could be so rude?! Here I was, on the adventure of a lifetime, raising money for charity, not doing any harm, and this campsite was so snooty! They couldn't even spare a small patch of grass and some water for me, which I would've been happy to pay for. I tried not to let it dampen my spirits, 99% of the people and campsites I'd come across so far had shown nothing but kindness. The majority of campsites had given me a discounted hikers rate and some had even let me stay for free. I'd only had this one and one other campsite turn me away.

I trudged my way further down the road, hoping to the universe that there was indeed another campsite. And sure enough, 50 metres later, I came across more than "just a field". Land's End Camping was a very cool looking place. Quite new it seemed, hence why it wasn't showing on my maps, with a luxurious newly built shower block and a wide open field of tents and van-dwellers, set against the backdrop of a large working dairy farm.

I was warmly greeted by the campsite owner, a bubbly guy in his 40s wearing surf shorts, a hoodie and a bumbag. He looked like a market stall holder at a festival. He showed me to my pitch and I told him about my unpleasant encounter with Seaview Campsite a few minutes before.

"Oh I know, my love, they are so horrible up there! I can't tell you how many times we've had people come to us saying how rude they are! Here, if you need a good giggle later once you're set up, have a look at their Google reviews. They are quite shocking."

"Ah haha that's good to know that I'm not the only one! I will for sure have a look at the reviews." I replied.

"And here you are, love, as you're hiking for charity, have TWO shower tokens instead of one. I don't normally do this but you look like you could use a nice long hot shower after those people were so rude to you!"

"Oh my goodness thank you so much, you didn't have to do that. I appreciate the kindness, thank you. I'll enjoy a nice long shower then, I do really need it actually. I would've come to you guys first if I'd known you were here!" I said beaming. Well this sure is so much better than Seaview! I thought to myself. I was actually glad they turned me away otherwise I would've never stumbled upon this magical place.

Shortly after I'd set up my tent and had a blissful shower, I thought about dinner. The temptation was too much. I'd spotted a fish'n'chips place along the road before the campsite and I just couldn't resist going back and treating myself. I skipped back along the road, my nose leading me to the warm, salty aroma of deep-fat-fryers. I ordered salt & pepper squid and a portion of chips with sweet chilli sauce on the side and practically sprinted back to the campsite.

When I got back, I saw that I'd been joined by another tiny tent and another long distance hiker inside it. A woman in her 30s, muscular and very experienced looking. We chatted about our journeys so far and she told me how she, too, was hiking the entire SWCP in one go. But she's doing it in reverse, starting at Poole and finishing at Minehead.
"Finally, another single woman is doing it like me!" I giggled with her. It seemed symbolic somehow that we'd met at Land's End, she just finishing the south coast, and I just finishing the north coast of the SWCP.

She looked longingly at my dinner.
"Go and get yourself some of this. You deserve it. And it's so. Damn. Good!" I persuaded her.
"Oh alright then, I don't need much convincing!" she said laughing as she got up to go and buy her treasure.

I tucked into mine. I swooned with pleasure. Tender strips of crispy squid, seasoned to perfection and not chewy at all. And classic chip-shop-chips doused in salt and vinegar so they were that ecstatic blend of crispy on the outside, fluffy on the inside, but kind of on the verge of soggy from the vinegar. And everything draped in a silky caress of sweet chilli sauce. I sighed with glee.

As I was getting lost in my foodie heaven, familiar faces rocked up at the campsite - it was Gemma and Adam who I met at Polzeath all the way back on day 13! I almost didn't recognise Adam, so engrossed was I in eating.
"India! So good to see you again! You've made it this far, well done! How are you doing?" he said with a big smile.
We excitedly caught up with each other and I regailed him with tales of my journey since we'd last met, and he filled me in on their progress. Turns out Adam and I had had similar foot injuries. Mine had healed ok now, but his was still aggravating him and his ankle was strapped up with industrial strength runner's tape. It was so good to see them again, feeling like they were my trail-brother-and-sister.

I settled into my tent for the evening just as a large group of male cyclists and their support vehicle set up camp and was contentedly lulled to sleep by excited talk of their long journey. I caught snippets of conversations and destinations achieved, "John O'Groats... London... we've made it to Land's End!... Well done chaps!... bloody hell I'm starving..."

I couldn't wait to see what more my own journey had to offer. I'd just completed day 24, I'd finished the northern side of the SWCP. Now, it was the longer stretch along the southern side. I wondered how the landscape would change. How the weather would change. So far, it has generally been pretty remote and wild. I was completely consumed by it. Eat, walk, sleep, repeat. I felt as though I could carry on forever.

Day 25, a full moon. I woke up and instantly felt a certain energy in the air. It was incredibly foggy, so much so that I could barely see more than five feet in front of me. I set off as early as I could, 7:30am, so I could miss the crowds at Land's End and get to the iconic landmark at 7:45am before anything was open. It had a very post-apocalyptic-like atmosphere. Overly cheerful amusement arcades and caricature statues that lay eerily still and quiet, shrouded in the blanket of mist that made them look more menacing than friendly. There was a kiosk next to the Land's End Signpost that stated one had to pay £10 to get a picture with it.

"£10?! For a picture with a signpost?!" I chuckled to myself at the ludicrousy of it. I hopped over the red rope barrier, bypassed the closed kiosk and felt quite smug as I took a selfie with the signpost on my phone, for free.

"Would you like me to take a picture of you?"
I span around. Shit. I've been caught!
"No point paying a tenner at this time of day,
hey!" said the kind woman with her grown up
daughter.
"Oh, thank you so much I'd really appreciate
that! I'm hiking the SWCP and just passing
through so I didn't see the point in paying either!
And besides, it's not even open yet... What are
you doing here at this time of day?" I replied,
curiosity piqued.
"Well, my husband is part of a big cycling group
and they are finishing here at Land's End today
so we're here early to welcome them across the
finishing line!"
"Ah yes! I heard them arrive at Land's End
Camping last night. Sounds like quite a journey
they've been on. Wish them congratulations
from me."
"I will, for sure. Ah well done you for doing this all
on your own! Stay safe out there yeah?" she said
as she took a picture of me with my phone. We
laughed as we realised there wasn't much of a
view as the fog was so thick you couldn't even
see the sea below the signpost. We said
goodbye and I disappeared into the mist.

Out of the Land's End tourist park, the path
rambled around lots of small coves and strange
rock formations. The fog was stubborn, showing
no signs of lifting and there was something
about the air. I could feel the pull of the full
moon so strongly. She was speaking to me, ever

so softly, from behind the shroud of grey dawn. A murmur so gentle I couldn't make it out yet. I felt cocooned in the embrace of the fog. Thick but not suffocating, womb-like, as I slowed down my pace and wandered through my wonderland.

Damp moss. Wet earth. Lapping waves. Growth. Something was brewing inside me with each step. With each breath of moist, cool air. The path was leading me to something... a release was about to happen. I could feel it in the lump forming in my throat, in the butterflies in my stomach, in the tingling of my spine and the raised hairs on the back of my neck.

And there it was.
The path led me down to the most perfect untouched beach. I chuckled at the name the stone plaque stated it was called: Nanjizel. Sounded like something Snoop Dogg would say. It was pristinely clean. No footprints, a blank slate washed clean by the fresh overnight tides. It was lined by a bank of large stone boulders and a set of steep rusty iron steps leading down to them. Once again, as before with my soul tree, my instincts took over. I took my pack off, set it down with care at the base of the steps and gingerly picked my way over the boulders until I finally reached the golden sand.

Beyond the sand was crystal clear turquoise water, rippling slightly with a light almost too bright considering the heaviness of the air above it, and beyond that was the fog, still so dense. To the right of me was a deep dark cave. It looked like a passage to another world... or maybe I was in that other world and the cave led back to civilization, technology and chaos.

I picked up one of my walking poles, walked over to the flattest part of the beach, calmly in a trance and wrote a message in the sand that came from deep within my soul.

I forgive you.
I release it all.
I am free.
I begin.

An epiphany. A letting go of a time before. Rebirth. Closure.

Tears spilled from my eyes in raw emotion. What that emotion was I couldn't really say. And then the tears stopped just as suddenly as they came. I felt peace at the fact that the ocean tide will come and wash those notes away. A clean slate.

I walked up into the cliffs and away from the beach, not once looking back, and finally the fog started to lift. By the time I reached the Minnack Theatre at midday it was a hot, bright, sunny day and the path was busy with tourists about to watch a show. I was beginning to get tired and wasn't fussed about seeing the theatre itself, promising to myself to visit and see a show one day. I carried on a couple miles more, eventually reached Treen Farm Campsite, a beautiful spot above the cliffs overlooking the sparkling big blue, and was greeted warmly at reception by the lady who ran it. The fat, fresh strawberries on the counter were too beautiful to resist and after I'd set my pitch up, I basked in the early afternoon sun and revelled in sucking on the plump red jewels of nature.

The sun began to set on the western horizon. Laying on the grass beside my tent, I'd watched it slowly sink all afternoon and now it was low enough that it paint-brushed the atmosphere with the golden red embers of its evening serenade. I felt a deep peacefulness after my release that morning. My life before this walk, all the pain, hurt and anger, a red ball of fiery anguish it once had been, now had the hazy hue of a melting sunset. A few final sparks of release came to me and I whispered them outloud into the sky, watching as they faded into the purple-blue, hoping that wherever he was, he would somehow hear me.

"I hope you have a good life."

"Thank you for everything you taught me."

I woke with renewed energy on the 26th day on my beloved path. It was raining lightly and my tent was heavy with morning dew which weighed my pack down with the extra water, as much as I tried to shake it off, but I set off feeling bright and breezy all the same.

The path leading out of Treen hugged the cliff tops and soon became a wild roller coaster of tight hedgerows and rocky outcrops. It was extremely overgrown, it seemed that no one had passed this section for quite a while and I struggled to hack my way through the thick jungle foliage.

"Oh good god! Ugggghh this is frustrating!" I wailed to the wind. There was so much wet foliage on the ground that seeped into my boots and soaked my socks as I brushed past them. I squelched on as the path became narrower and narrower. The hedges became taller and taller until I felt like Alice in Wonderland after she'd taken the shrinking potion. Deep dark tunnels of bracken, bramble and bush battered me. The path, which seemed like it hadn't seen daylight in a hundred years, became a soup of brown sludge.

Oh shit. There in front of me was a deep, long slushy bog with a thousand blue bottle flies swarming around a rotting husk of bark protruding from the centre. There was no way around it. The canopy of thick jungle was all encompassing on every side of me.

"Euuuurrgh oh no no nooo..." I groaned to myself. Nothing for it but to go through. I reached my foot out wide to try and place it on the rotting bark so I'd at least have something to stand on instead of sinking right down into the mud. Almost there... yes... just a little farther... ah... yes! I'd planted my first foot on the bark, now I just had to transfer my weight, get the other foot on and tiptoe along it like a tightrope to reach the other side of the bog. Well, that was the plan anyway.

Flies. Rotting bark. Wet sludge. Decay hung in the air at that moment. Time slowed and a stench of death rose from the pit and filled my nostrils with a foreboding that perhaps I always knew was coming. Here goes... I started to transfer my weight... but then-

SWOOP!

A moment of shock. Like when a child falls and there's that moment of silence before all hell breaks loose.

"AAAAUUUUUURRRRRRGGGGGHHHHH!!!!" I burst into hot tears of anger. I'd almost made it fully onto the oasis of bark amongst the bog, but I'd slipped and landed in the stinking swamp and was now sitting in a pool of brown misery wailing like a five year old. I had a full-blown tantrum. A full-on ego death as a wave of embarrassment and self-pity came screaming out of my eyes and mouth in unintelligible rants of swears and curses.

I'm not sure how long I wallowed there for... five minutes? Half an hour? Or maybe just 30 seconds... Eventually I heaved myself out of the pit and squelched on, my pride well and truly diminished.
"Fucking bastard swamp.... Fucking path... fucking foliage fuck-shitting-twat-pissing-shitbag.." I mumbled to myself as I carried on battling through the jungle, my leggings sticking to me and stinking as if I'd shit myself... had I?

I came to a boulder perfectly shaped to sit on and took my shoes and socks off. I squeezed them, wrung them out one by one as a gush of stinking brown soup drained from them. I tried my best to squeeze as much liquid out as possible but when I put my shoes and socks back on, they didn't really feel much different.

The path continued its relentless torture and my shoes and socks instantly filled with water coming from the low lying grasses again. I repeated wringing them out again and again, the flesh on my feet becoming milky white and wrinkled. Boulder after swamp after thick foliage after boulder after jungle. For miles I wailed and swore and growled. I was growling over one such rocky outcrop when a young shiny couple in their 20s with spotless brand-new hiking clothes passed me and jumped in fright. I burst out laughing, cackling like a maniac as I realised how crazy I must've seemed and they looked at me even weirder as they hurriedly scuttled past. "Be careful the path is really fucking overgrown back there!" I yelled at their backs, heckling like an old swamp witch. I could only imagine what a fright I did look like... covered in mud, sweat and foliage, hair sticking up all over the place with the look of a rabid dog in my eyes.

At last! Oh sweet joy! A café! I'd finally reached the little cove of Lamorna and burst through the café doors like a bull in a china shop; starving, ravenous for something hot and filling. I was greeted by a cute guy behind the counter. He was around my age with long curly blonde hair tied up in a messy bun and a goatee beard. "Hey, wow you look like you could use a cup of tea and a sit down! What can I get you, darling?" he said.
"Hey! Oh yes, I've had a bloody frustrating morning... Can I please have a cup of earl grey tea? Ooh and that vegan pasty there please... ooh and do you have wifi? I just need to check in with my family." I blushed at him.
"Sure you can. We don't have wifi here but you can use the hotspot on my phone if you like. My name's Jon by the way." Jon said. He had a little glint in his eye, a little frisson of something passing between us.

I started to calm down as I enjoyed the delicious tea and pasty, chatting to Jon and the middle aged couple sitting opposite me about my journey so far. I was feeling rather magnetic as I regaled them with stories of my triumphs and despairs and as I got up to leave, Jon handed me a slip of paper with his phone number on.

"Hey India... I live in Penzance so when you're passing through... maybe give me a call and you can have a night in my place if you want to? Only if you want to though... y'know if you want a shower or to use my washing machine or something..." he said, that twinkle in his eye again.
"Aw Jon... thank you, that's really sweet of you... yeah maybe..." I replied vaguely. I didn't come on this walk to meet a guy. He was cute but I knew we'd be just passing ships in the night. I wanted to stay focused and complete this thing. Nothing was going to get in my way.

I carried on out of Lamorna and the path continued up and down steep valleys. Still so overgrown, wet and rocky, but at least the swamps were a thing of the past now. I was exhausted. The physical effort of battling through the last 10 miles wiped me out and by the time I hobbled into Mousehole (pronounced Mousle) I was hunched over my walking poles, thighs trembling from fatigue, soggy feet reeking of decay.

Mum came rushing up to me when she saw the state I was in. She was visiting me for a resupply and decided to be my back-up vehicle for the weekend. She'd come prepared and the boot of her silver Ford Focus was packed with her own tent, camping supplies and bags of food.

"Oh darling! Oh my goodness look at you, oh my love, you look terrible!"

"Ugggghhhh Mum that was so awful! I've had a horrible day, it was so hard!" tears pricked in my eyes as she hugged me.

"Ooh... yes I can smell it, my love... phew, you need a shower!"

"Sniff... haha... well thanks... I guess?" I snivelled into her lovely ambergris scented maternal shoulder.

We drove a mile inland to Mousehole Football Club & Campsite and just managed to pitch our tents before another spot of rain arrived. The shower block was heavenly. I stood under the jet of steaming water and leaned my head against the PVC-tile wall as my body was soothed and cleansed from the day. Dried mud, dried blood, dried leaves swished away from my skin. The skin on my feet, now almost translucent and as wrinkled as prunes, breathed a sigh of relief at no longer being imprisoned in a wet cage of brown liquid.

Mum cooked a slap up meal on the camping stove of pesto pasta with peas and boiled eggs and I devoured every bite as usual. I felt so grateful once again to have such an incredible support network around me. Tomorrow is another day, I thought. More urban according to my guidebook, which I felt surprising relief at. I fell asleep quickly and deeply.

Day 27. Mum and I packed up camp and drove back down to Mousehole town centre where she dropped me off, said goodbye and headed off towards Praa Sands, 12 miles down the line where I'd be meeting her at the end of the day. It was all concrete flat walking today, a welcome change from the trials of yesterday. The weather was fine and cool with a gentle breeze. Just pleasant.

Mousehole to Newlyn to Penzance to Marazion to Praa Sands - all very quaint fishing hubs with pretty cottages, harbours, boats, beaches and pubs. All rolled by gently as I steamed past on the concrete seaside walkway that connects them all. I didn't stop to explore these towns. I pushed on through, making mental notes to visit again one day and explore them properly.

Jon and I had sent a couple platonic messages to each other. But nothing will come of it. I don't want it. I just want to be with myself right now. I am the love of my life. I am fulfilling my dreams. Just me and my pack, out here on an adventure. I whooped into the breeze as I strolled along the promenade, feeling as free as the seabirds swirling on the current above me.

I met Mum at Praa Sands 12 miles later, but feeling like I'd done 6. It passed by in a flash today, I felt energised and satisfied. Praa Sands looked pretty much just like one big caravan park, but we found a cute little place called Pentreath Farm Campsite to stay in for the night. A field with a toilet and shower block high up in the hills, it was rustic, but just perfect for what we needed.

The air was heavy and I smelled rain on the horizon. As I settled into my tent for the evening, I felt tired, but satisfied on the fairly uneventful day. I marvelled at how this life had consumed me. Even today, uneventful as it was, almost mundane in its routine, still felt spectacular and awe inspiring.

Day 28 and Mum and I woke to cold, heavy rain. We sheltered in the shower block of the campsite as we cooked on the campstove, ate our breakfast of bacon and eggs on toast and giggled at how ridiculous it must've looked. Today I was headed for the little town of Mullion, where Mum will meet me at day's end. I couldn't thank her enough for her company this weekend. A welcome morale boost after a tiring and wet week. However old I get, whatever being a "grown-up" means, a girl will always need her Mum. And I felt so thankful to have her.

Catherine Hicks is a force of nature in itself. She is Mother Nature. Fiercely independent and strong-willed. Witty, funny and beautiful with long curly brown-blonde hair down to her waist. Petit, but you notice her presence as soon as she walks into a room. She taught me what unconditional love is. When my brother and I were ages 10 and 12, she, together with my Dad, scooped us up and saved us from a life of judgement and servitude within a hypocritical religion and turned her back on everything she had known for the past 40 years. Despite the turmoil she must've felt at going through a divorce, leaving a religion, leaving a toxic community, she did everything she could to protect my brother and I. Not once did we ever feel doubtful of her love. Even throughout the following years when she was trying to discover who she was, getting in and out of bad relationships with men that treated her like shit, all the arguments we had during my tricky teen years, my constant worry at the path she was going down, I never once doubted her love.

I said goodbye to her in the car park in Praa Sands.
"See you 11 miles down the line!" she said.
"Thank you, Mum. Really." I replied, sincerely.
"Oh darling, do you know, I'm actually loving being your support vehicle this weekend - I'm having a little exploration journey of Cornwall for myself! I love you!" she said as she waved and drove away.

"I love you too!" I said, waving back.

Today I was heading to the little town of Mullion, made famous by the Italian inventor Guglielmo Marconi, who invented the first wireless radio transmission that ran from there to America in 1901.

It was pouring down with rain as I trudged along the wet beach at Praa Sands. Once again, I battled with the dilemma of keeping my waterproof trousers on but my legs getting moist and sweaty inside them, or taking them off and getting them wet with rain anyway. The same with my waterproof jacket. It didn't take long before I got too hot in the suffocating fabric and stripped off anyway.

"Ahhhhhhh..." I sighed sweet relief as the plump droplets of rain sizzled and splashed against my hot skin. I'd just climbed to the top of the cliff past the beach, slipped my pack from my back, peeled off my sodden waterproofs and shook off my fleece and t-shirt.

I stood, half naked, with my eyes closed, my face towards the rumbling grey sky, my arms outstretched wide, giggling with lust for this beautiful life.

Misty vapour rose off me, but some bigger droplets stayed, trickling down my arms and neck, pooling in my palms and collar bone.

Water ran down my face and chest, down my stomach, down my thighs in an explosion of hot and cold sensuality.

I opened my mouth. Tasted the rain. Tasted the wonder of the universe. The source of life itself.

Everything became a state of flow. The crashing waves, the rolling clouds, the blood coursing through my veins, the wind swirling around my waist as if we were dancing the waltz. "WOOOOOOOO!!" I cried into the electric ether.

The path undulated over many quiet little coves and beaches today as my footsteps strode effortlessly through it. Over craggy black cliffs, grassy headland, old stone mining buildings and the wildness of the Lizard Peninsula. Moss and heather was abundant around me, soaking up the torrent of water falling from above. I could not have been more wet. My waterproofs, my clothes, my kit, my body, I may as well have been swimming in the sea to Mullion. And I loved it. I felt so alive with awareness. With feeling. Every sense heightened with exhilaration and pleasure.

I came across more swollen patches of grass beside the path that jiggled and sloshed about like a water balloon when I jumped on them, which had me roaring with laughter. As people were sheltering in their houses, and birds were sheltering in their trees, I was in my element amongst the elements. A wild woman in her house of divinity. A goddess of nature playing in her sacred garden.

Eventually I rounded one particular corner of a rocky cliff and made my way inland to Mullion town centre. The heavy rain had not ceased all day and when Mum saw me sheltering briefly under a shopfront selling bodyboards and sunglasses, she gasped, a look of amused horror on her face.

"Ind!!! You must be freezing! Are you alright, love?! Oh my god, right, wait a minute, I think I need to put some towels down in the car."

"Haha Mum, I'm fine. I'm more than fine. I'm amazing! I loved it today." I replied, getting into the passenger seat after shaking off like a wet dog as best I could.

"I've had a look on the map, Mum, and there's a campsite we could stay in tonight not far from here. Looks like some sort of farm-campsite. Shall I give them a call unless you've got any other ideas?" I suggested.

"That sounds good darling, let's find somewhere quick before it gets dark."

I gave the farm a call, it didn't have a name on the map, just a green tent symbol and a phone number, a seed of hesitation popped in my mind, but I pressed dial anyway.

"H'llo." came a gruff middle aged man's voice.

"Oh, yes, hello... um... is this the right number for the campsite?" I said, unsure whether I'd got the right number.

"Sniff... yeah, sure."

"... o-okay... Well, do you have any space for two tents and a small car for tonight, please?" he's being a bit weird, I thought.

"Hff... yeah, sure. Meet you at the gate." he said with all the enthusiasm of a piece of cardboard.

"Ah, great, um, thanks, we'll see you in about ten min-" I said, not quite finishing my sentence before he hung up.

"Are we ok then, love?" Mum said.

"Uhhh yeah I think so... the guy sounded a bit weird though... let's check it out anyway and if we don't like it we can always turn back." I said.

The heavy rain still did not cease as we winded down country lanes that seemed to get narrower and narrower. The map led us down an incredibly bumpy gravel track that seemed like it hadn't been maintained for quite some time with long grasses sticking up everywhere and overgrown hedges either side of the car. At the end of the gravel track was a heavy metal farm gate with a tatty greying wooden sign saying "camping" sloppily painted on it. It looked like something out of a horror movie - was that red paint or blood?

"I think this is the place... It must be..." I said as Mum shot me a look of unease.

I got out of the car, opened the gate, Mum drove to the other side and I hopped back in before I got soaked again.

"Well... this is... rustic?" Mum said half laughing and half gasping in shock.

What we had driven into was quite possibly the most basic "campsite" ever to have existed. An overgrown field with one small wooden shack housing a long drop toilet and no other sign of civilization apart from a dilapidated caravan covered in dark green mould. The scene looked even more menacing with the heavy rain and dark thundering clouds.

"Mum... ooh, I don't like this. I don't like this at all, I'm getting really bad vibes from this place." I said, shivering as I imagined the man on the phone holding us hostage in the mouldy caravan and torturing us.

"Ooh, me too Ind... hey let's get out of here quick before the man comes!" she squealed.

And with that, we spun around and drove away from that place as fast as we could as if our life depended on it, breathing deep sighs of relief that we didn't see anyone there. We decided to drive to Henry's Campsite at Lizard town. I hadn't planned to stay there until I reached Lizard Point the following day, but we decided after the encounter we'd just had, that two nights at the legendary Henry's Campsite would be just what was needed. This would be the last night I'd spend with Mum before she leaves to go home in the morning.

As soon as we rounded the hill and began winding down into Lizard Town, the clouds lightened, the rain ceased and the sun coyly began to peak through. It was the perfect welcoming party.

We drove into Henry's Campsite with mouths agog at the lush Caribbean-like oasis we'd just discovered. To the right of the driveway lay an open teepee-shaped canvas canopy with large comfy sofas, armchairs, cushions and persian rugs. An old piano and giant oak coffee table lay centred amongst the furniture and fairy lights adorned the edges of the canopy. Chickens and ducks pecked their way around freely whilst to the left of the driveway stood a shower and toilet block made of rustic pieces of plywood and pallet, painted in a rainbow of vibrant hues.

The husband and wife owners welcomed us with open arms and showed us to our spot for the night, their lively children hanging off their arms like little monkeys. Each camping pitch was like its own little private grove lined with tropical palm trees, foxgloves and other exotic flora I didn't know the name of. Our one was nestled in a quiet corner behind a line of lush hedgerow.

After we'd set up camp, Mum and I wandered into the town centre to see where we could grab a bite to eat. We came across The Witchball Pub and dived in before another rain shower hit.

Behind the counter a very charming guy in his early twenties welcomed us in and served us a drink. He had that smooth-operator maverick-look in his eyes that both intrigued and slightly cringed me. We got talking about what I was doing and before I knew what was happening he was giving me his card and inviting me out for a drink after his shift finished! Mum and I sat down to eat.

"So, are you going to meet him after his shift then?!" she whispered excitedly, trying to play matchmaker.

"Mmm not sure. Maybe? I guess it could just be fun?" I said, feeling like a total badass boss babe.

After our dinner of hearty pub grub, which of course I gobbled down at lightning speed, Mum wandered back down to the campsite and I stayed out and had a drink with charming-bar-guy. Just water. It had been a long time since I'd had alcohol and I didn't want anything clouding my senses on this adventure. We got to know each other, talking about our spiritual journeys, our lives, our likes and dislikes. He complimented me on my smile, my eyes, my aura. My stomach started to flutter a little. Why does this feel like a date? I wondered. But then. He let slip that he had a girlfriend back home waiting for him.

The balloon of excitement suddenly popped and deflated, the red flags were flying. So... he's got a girlfriend... but he invited me out for a drink?
"OK, this feels a bit weird now..." I said.
"Hmm. Maybe... I've had a really nice time with you though... Would you like me to drive you back round to the campsite? I mean... not in a weird way... just to get you back safe y'know? It's getting dark." he replied.
"Ok... that's thoughtful of you, thank you." I said.
Careful India, my intuition whispered to me.

It was only a 30 second drive around the corner to Henry's Campsite. Charming-bar-guy pulled up outside as promised and dropped me off.
"Well. Thanks for dropping me back. It was lovely meeting you." I said, genuinely. It actually had been lovely to meet him. We'd seemingly had a lot in common and he was very interesting.
"The pleasure was all mine, India." He replied, looking intently into my eyes.
A pause. I cut it off.
We exchanged a brief hug goodbye and I swiftly got out of his car. Turning back just once to wave him off, feeling glad that I was back in the campsite.

"So, how was it?!?! You're back earlier than I thought?!" Mum asked, wide eyed, as I returned to our little corner.
"He's got a girlfriend. Was nice to meet him though." I replied nonchalantly with a shrug.
"Oh. Bit of a playboy do you think?"

"Mmm, not sure. I actually don't think so... I think he was just genuinely charming and clearly very friendly. I think I just got the wrong end of the stick." I said yawning and crawling into my tent.
"Well, it's always nice to meet new people isn't it, darling? Night night. I love you."
"Love you too, Mum. Night night."

Day 29. Mum and I woke up together for the last time on this trip and she cooked a big breakfast on the camping stove. We packed her things away in the car but left my tent and kit set up for another night, meaning I could enjoy today's walk with just my day pack. Today she was going to drop me back to Mullion where I left off yesterday and I would walk the eight miles back here to Henry's Campsite and enjoy a second night in this lovely spot. I was fully restocked with supplies for another week and felt satisfied.

"Mum. Thank you, thank you, thank you. It's meant so much to me to have your support this weekend." I said with tears in my eyes.
"Oh my darling. You are so welcome. You know I'd do anything for you, my baby girl. I'm so proud of you." she said, tears welling from her eyes too. We gave each other the biggest bear hug outside the public loos at Mullion. And then she was off, back to civilization. And I carried on, here in my wild.

The walk around the Lizard Peninsula today was refreshing and easy. The torrential rain from yesterday had ceased, leaving behind a diluted wash of grey in the watercolour sky. The breeze was gentle yet bracing and I power-walked around stubby grassy headlands teeming with nesting birds. Little wildflower meadows provided abundant nourishment for hundreds of bumblebees. And a few rocky cliffs gave way to bubbling rivers which I leap-frogged across.

My inner child sang and laughed as I played in MY Garden of Eden. There was no forbidden fruit here. No wrath of a single judgmental deity. No constructed false hierarchy. Only abundance. Only acceptance. Only joy. Only peace. Unconditional love.

It was lunchtime and I'd already hiked the eight miles back to Henry's Campsite, so I decided to spend the afternoon resting, reading through my SWCP Guidebook and maps for the thousandth time, journaling and snuggling up in the hippie outside lounge area amongst the persian rugs and old squishy sofas that almost consumed me as I sank down into one of them.

My eyes began to droop by mid afternoon so I made my way back to my tent, made an early dinner and decided to get an early night in. As I'd just started to drift off, I heard familiar voices outside my tent. A man and a woman's voice debriefing their day's hike and what they had planned for tomorrow.

"Gemma! Adam! I thought that was you! It's so good to see you, how are you guys?!" I said excitedly, popping my head out of my tent.
"India! We thought that was your little tent! We recognised it straight away!" Gemma replied with a big smile.
We instantly got to talking about our journeys since we'd last caught each other at Land's End. It felt like catching up with my trail-brother-and-sister. Kindred spirits who really understood the journey and all the ups and downs our beloved path provided.

That night I slept soundly. My body is used to sleeping on my thin thermal mat now. One of my last thoughts before sleep claimed me was how it would feel strange when eventually I would return to a normal bed.

Week 5 – First Nature

Day 30. My one month trail-anniversary! I couldn't believe it. On the one hand it felt like I was only just getting started, getting stronger everyday. And on the other hand, I could scarcely remember a time before my walk, it was second nature to me now.

Today's route passed through some pretty challenging terrain, but mostly absolutely gorgeous, interesting and enchanting. Setting off from The Lizard, the path undulated, at times becoming lofty with cliffs, but nuggets of tranquillity lay in tiny fishing hamlets nestled in quiet valleys. I paused for a granola bar mid-morning on a crooked wooden bench that had an excellent view point to a most interesting rock formation called, according to my map, Devil's Frying Pan. It was a milky turquoise lagoon encircled by two tall jagged cliffs. And connecting these two cliffs was a naturally forming black rock bridge topped with grass and heather. I could see why it was named as it was, it could be both beautiful and terrifying if one were to get caught in the cove at high tide.

I carried on rambling up and down the scruffy scraggy cliff tops.
"Bloody hell! Oof! Up we go! Come on India!" I encouraged myself. For some reason, this section in particular had an incredible amount of

flights of steps. Stone plates unevenly protruding out of the bedrock that a clumsy giant seemed to have made. They were so tall and I could barely reach one step to another with my little legs. My walking poles provided valuable traction to hoist myself up these giant-steps. I affirmed to myself that I definitely wouldn't have been able to climb them had it not been for my poles.

Eventually I dragged my now very wobbly legs around to Coverack, a beautiful, totally picturesque seaside village nestled amongst tall cliffs, and began to climb up the steep tarmac road to Little Trevothen Campsite, my finish line for the day. When I got there and checked into reception, the lovely young chap who owned it with his parents gave me a cup of tea, "on the house!" he said, and a deckchair to sit on. "You're the second SWCP hiker staying here today! Nice couple called up earlier and booked their slot so they should be along soon." he said. "Ooh, by any chance, are they called Adam and Gemma? They are my friends that I've made along the way!"
"Haha yes that's them! Ah, I'll make sure to put them in the pitch next to yours then!" he said kindly.
"Aw thank you so much, this is such a lovely spot you've got here." I said, looking around with wide eyes.

Little Trevothen Campsite is about a mile inland from Coverack. It's a cosy yet neat spot, excellently maintained with really pretty surroundings. The main campground itself is cocooned with pine trees, with a single line of tall trees dividing the centre, offering privacy and shelter. I'd set up my tent, the tent poles effortlessly sliding into the perfectly firm grassy earth, set out my belongings and relaxed into my deck chair with my cup of tea and the pan-au-chocolat I'd bought from the little campsite shop.

"Ahhh, bliss." I said out loud, closing my eyes as the hot sweet tea warmed me from the inside out. The weather today had been cool, but the sunshine had come out for the late afternoon and was now gently caressing my cheeks in a warm glow. I opened my eyes and grinned as my trail-brother-and-sister strolled into view.
"Hey guys! How did you find it today?"
"Phew, pretty tiring… Adam's ankle is playing up again, isn't it honey?" Gemma said, furrowing her brow.
"Eeesh yeah… I'm grinning and bearing it to be honest… I think it's something that'll be with me for the rest of the trip…" Adam said grimacing as he released his aching feet from their walking-boot shackles.
"Aww ouchy… hey Adam, I've got a lightweight rubber ball in my bag that I've been using for my feet - why don't you have a go on it? I've found it really helpful for me." I offered.

Since my own foot injury, I'd been carrying a small blue rubber ball the size of a tennis ball around and using it to massage and roll along my feet everyday to prevent getting injured again. This simple trick had proven essential for me now and gave me so much relief at the end of the day.

"Ah that's great thanks, India. I'll give it a go tonight." he replied, legs stretched out on the grass.

Adam, Gemma and I continued sharing stories as we cooked our ration dinners on our camping stoves. The sun was setting and cast a golden-hour hue around us as we laughed and chatted and compared notes. I felt such a deep contentment in that moment to be around my fellow hikers. My tribe. My people. I realised that I'd had a chronic lack of community these past few years. But this year, as soon as I'd started to look inward and heal what was happening inside, I attracted everything I'd longed for on the outside.

That night, I had probably the best night's sleep I'd had on my trip so far. Snuggling down into my caterpillar-green sleeping bag, curled up on my silver thermal mat with my head gently resting on my blue blow-up pillow, sheltered in my khaki-green cocoon, my wings began to grow. Just fluttering, there around my heart, they were ready to burst through and fly.

Day 31. I woke up, well rested, to warm pleasant sunshine brushing over my tent and got up quickly, eager to make the most of it. I could hear Adam and Gemma still sound asleep below their orange canvas dome so I was careful to make my movements slow and gentle whilst eating breakfast and packing up my things so as not to wake them. I hopped briefly over to the toilet block, did my morning routine: brush teeth, go to the loo, wash face, sunscreen, sunscreen, sunscreen. Backpack on, strapped in, walking poles in hand. Ready.

I wandered back down the road to Coverack village centre and stopped briefly to take in the utter exquisiteness of what lay before me. The rising sun sparkled over the calm lapping water below the tiny fishing harbour. Shiny yachts and small rowing boats bobbed about happily whilst seabirds floated on by them. And the whitewashed houses just started to make hushed noises, waking up for another day in tranquillity. It looked like a scene from a James Bond film and I felt as though I'd stepped into a village on the Italian Amalfi Coast.

Today, all being well, I would reach the SWCP halfway marker which, according to my guidebook, is located at Porthallow. My heart fluttered with excitement and I promised myself to get a picture with it to update my family. Walking out of Coverack, the path was nothing short of classic pretty English countryside.

Flourishing little woodlands, lowland coves, chirping birds and delicate flowers swaying in the soft summer breeze.

In one such woodland, I came across the legendary Fat Apples Café, popular with weary hikers, and decided to treat myself to a pasty. I sat in their garden on a picnic bench under the teepee canvas and had a delicious vegan spiced chickpea pasty with sweet red onion relish and salad drizzled with a mustard and olive oil dressing. All washed down with a crisp ginger beer. I closed my eyes and couldn't help but do a little happy dance at the explosion of flavours in my eager mouth.

"The food is so good here, isn't it?" came a man's voice a few feet away.

I opened my eyes and saw that the voice belonged to a fellow long distance hiker. He was tall, probably mid forties with a kind face, rectangular glasses and of course all the necessary kit for a thru-hike that I instantly recognised. He was studying what looked to be a guidebook, but I saw had lots of handwritten notes and annotations on.

"Mmm SO good! Hey, you must be hiking the coast path as well? How much are you doing?" I replied.

"Yes I am! Well I work as a freelance writer for a travel company and they wanted me to update their guidebook on South Cornwall's section of the SWCP, so I thought why not make it a proper trip, camp and actually do the hiking in real-time! What about you?" he said.

"Oh wow that's amazing! Sounds like the perfect job! I'm India by the way, I'm hiking all 630 miles in one go. Reaching the halfway point today!" I said excitedly.

"Good on you! What an incredible adventure! My name's Daniel. Hey, I think I remember seeing you at the Lizard actually?"

"Oh yes me too, I remember seeing you! Well, it was lovely to meet you properly, I'll bump into you again I'm sure over the next few days. Enjoy your lunch." I said, finishing my mouthful and hoisting my pack on just as Daniel's food was brought to his table by the waitress.

"Yes, I will see you down the line for sure. Nice to meet you too, India!"

Belly satisfied, I carried on towards Porthallow. The path had been recently diverted due to a landslip and followed winding country roads down the valley, through lush farmland and eventually down into the little fishing hub that marked the halfway point of the SWCP. I walked through the main street, got to the tiny beach harbour to rejoin the coast path and stood in front of a 6ft tall rectangular granite monument. It had a poem about nature on it, but no indication as to whether it was the actual halfway monument. I looked around in puzzlement.

"Hmm. I wonder where this marker could be? Surely this poem isn't it? There's no distance or mileage facts on there? I don't see any other markers around?" I said to myself, sweating in the midday sun, hands resting on the hip belt of my pack.

"Maybe it's a bit further on..." I mumbled to myself again, glancing at the steep incline hugging the clifftop out of Porthallow.

I carried on, eyes peeled for this elusive halfway marker, until two miles later, the penny dropped in my ditzy brain. I burst out half laughing, half wailing at my own airheadedness as I realised I'd not even thought to look around the other side of the marker, where the distance facts were probably stated.

"Ohhh, India! Agh, I can't be bothered to go all the way back just to get a picture! Pahaha... well this'll make a good anecdote I guess... so I got to the halfway marker.. but missed it entirely... duhhh!" I consoled myself.

Further down the path, I reached a gorgeous little hamlet called Gillan. Completed with thatched roof housing, lush floral gardens, tall old forests and private river moorings with cute little rowing boats. It had a creek that, during low tide one could paddle across using stepping stones to get to the other side. It was in between low and high tide when I got there so I took my pack off on the shingle beach, tore off my shoes and socks and sat down for an hour, waiting for the water levels to go down and basking in the mid afternoon sun.

"Hey India! We thought we might catch you at this point!"

I craned my neck around and grinned as Adam and Gemma came trudging over the shingle towards me.

"Hey guys! I hoped I might see you here too! We've just gotta wait for low tide to be able to cross. I think I just about see the stepping stones start to appear over there?" I said pointing to the bubbling river about ten feet away.

"Yep, I see it too. We've probably got another 20ish minutes to wait I reckon. India, have you thought about where you're going to camp tonight? We've been trying to research a campsite nearby but there doesn't seem to be anything around." Gemma said as they both joined me in taking their packs, shoes and socks off, letting sweaty feet breathe.

"Yes, I'd discovered that too. I thought I'd fill up with plenty of water at that pub at Helford Passage a bit later and then find somewhere to wild-camp in the fields beyond. Hey, do you guys mind if I camp with you tonight? We could all find a spot together?" I said, planting a seed of hope that I wouldn't have to wild-camp alone. I didn't mind doing it, but I'd rather be amongst friends if the opportunity arose.

"Of course, India! That would be really nice actually. Hey, let's have dinner together at that pub then as well if there's space." Gemma replied, Adam eagerly agreeing at the prospect of a pub dinner.

For the following half an hour, the three of us continued to compare notes about our experiences so far, Adam regaled us with stories from his travels in Asia and Gemma spoke more about her physio career. At around four o'clock, the tide was just low enough that we could roll our leggings up and begin to make the way across Gillan Creek. We discovered that the stepping stones weren't really of much use at all. They were covered in super slippery seaweed and it was much safer to wade carefully across the pebble river bed, the water coming up to our calves. The cold, refreshing river water felt heavenly as it ran through my legs. I stopped every so often to just stand there and enjoy the feeling of it.

After making it to the other side of the river and drying off, we continued to walk the rest of the day together, through more lush woodland that at times felt like hacking through a dense jungle.

At last, 14 miles on from where we began at Coverack and a short ferry trip across Helford Passage River, we were now seated in the riverside pub garden of the Ferryboat Inn that overlooked the busy river teeming with all kinds of boats, birds, human-life and wildlife. Adam had a pint of lager in his hand, Gemma had a white wine and I had a ginger beer and we continued getting to know each other deeper as the sun began to drop lower in the sky.

Our huge dinners came - burgers and generous helpings of chips - and conversation suddenly lulled as we concentrated on tucking into our precious meal. They understood fully how I felt about mealtimes at the moment. They knew exactly how important food was, how it was pretty much one of the only things we could ever think about when doing such an enormous task such as this walk. The silence only broke from time to time when one of us would exclaim ecstatic moans of "MMMMM!!" and "YUMMMMY!" at the sweet relief our grumbling stomachs felt.

The food comas set in pretty quickly after dinner and we joked about just laying down right here and now on the pub benches and sleeping here for the night. Alas, that couldn't be the case, so we heaved our packs back on and set off up into the hills to find somewhere to wild-camp. It was around 7pm, the evening was drawing in and we were all eager to find somewhere sooner rather than later. We passed what could've been the perfect camp spot in a little thicket of trees beside the path above some low cliffs, but there was already someone camping there. I wondered if it was Daniel. I didn't want to disturb the occupant by trying to find out.

We carried on staggering through the hills and farmland, everything a bit too exposed, or a bit too hilly, not flat enough, too much cow poo, too

much sheep poo, until two and a half miles later
we gave up and pitched our tents, 9:30pm at
night, at the bottom of a farming field where
cows had recently been. The ground was soft
with long lush grass and I fell asleep quickly,
after saying goodnight to my dear friends, on
the cushioned ground beneath me. My final
thoughts of the day drifted by contentedly. I
walked 16 miles in total, my best day yet! I felt
totally wiped out, but so proud of myself. I
drifted into unconsciousness whilst massaging
my legs out. Feeling the hardened, strong
muscles that hadn't been there a month ago,
but were now superwoman pieces of flesh. I
want to walk forever.

Day 32. Adam, Gemma and I woke up with the
sunrise and got packing up as soon as we could
so as not to get discovered by curious cows or
disgruntled farmers. I waved goodbye and
steamed ahead of them, eager to get started on
what looked set to be a beautifully sunny day.
The walk was beautiful and easy this morning as
the path meandered leisurely over low lying
coves and lush grassy headland. Strolling down
into the little hamlet of Maenporth, I couldn't
resist getting a chai latte and a sausage bap
from the beachfront café there.

As always, it was an ecstatic experience to eat.
Biting into the fluffy, yeasty bun housing salty,
meaty sausages caressed in lashings of ketchup
that went oozing down my chin like a silk glove

cupping my face. And then, I sipped on the sweet, cinnamony, spicy nectar of the goddess that is a chai latte. My absolute favourite beverage of all time. I giggled and closed my eyes to the sunrise as I appreciated my morning ritual.

I carried on up into the low cliffs to Falmouth. This next section of the path was super easy, flat, well maintained with tarmac and busy with tourists and local dog walkers alike. I walked through the pretty port of Falmouth with its charming old houses, indie shops, bustling harbour and bunting adorned streets and promised myself to visit again in the future and explore the area in more detail. After that, it was a short ferry ride across the river Fal to the little town of St Mawes and then a smaller ferry ride across the Percuil River to St Anthony's Church. From St Antony's Church it was a pleasant and easy walk around St Antony's Head and up the coast to Portscatho.

The sun beat down from a cloudless sky and the last couple miles I did struggle, breathing heavy sighs of relief whenever I passed through a shaded section of trees. It was so hot today, and when I finally reached Treloan Coastal Holidays campsite, after a 10 mile hike, in the green hills above Portscatho at around 4pm, I groaned as I slipped my pack from my back and could finally let my soaking lower back breath. I took my t-shirt off and wrung it out with salty sweat, did the same with my socks which hummed with a very strong musky odour. Then grasped at my water bottle to keep my demanding body hydrated as much as possible.

For the rest of the day I relaxed in my tent, breathing deep the delicious scent of the sea in the summer air. It really is a delicious scent. An aroma that so many companies have tried to bottle up and sell, but they can never come close to replicating the special magic that Mother Nature holds at her source. It's salty yet sweet, tangy yet mellow, warm yet so refreshing that to be surrounded by it is to be enveloped in the most tantalising sensation...
"What is that sensation?" I mused aloud as my head rested gently on my blow up pillow and my fingers toyed with the soft grass beneath me, my eyes drinking in the expanse of crystal blue above me.

Freedom.

That's it. That is the sensation. It's something unmarketable. Unsellable. And it lives within all of us. If only we choose to dive deep, trek through the muddy swamp of our shadows and embrace the clean air on the other side.

Day 33.
"Hey, India!"
I spun around as I walked out of the Treloan campsite entrance and a big grin spread across

my face as I saw my buddy Daniel coming up the road behind me.

"Hey, Daniel! Good to see you! How have you found it these past couple days? Hey, was that you wild camping just outside Helford Passage the other night?" I replied.

Daniel confirmed that it was indeed him in the little tent Gemma, Adam and I walked past that night and we proceeded to debrief each other on our journeys since.

"I'm just nipping into this campsite to update the guidebook so I'll see you further down the path today probably!" he said as we waved goodbye.

It was another beautifully sunny, hot day today and my route today along the path was pretty strenuous. I sweated buckets as I heaved myself and my pack up and down steep hills, my arms using all their muscles to propel myself forward with my walking poles. After a few miles I took a break at a cute little café at a tiny cove I didn't know the name of. It wasn't quite yet open so I patiently waited outside the gate, ticking the seconds away until it was 10am and I could get my fill of a soothing cup of tea and a pasty. As I waited, sure enough, Daniel came galloping down the hill.

"Hey Daniel! I didn't think it would take you long to catch me up!"

"Hello again India, ooh are you waiting for the café to open? Good idea, I fancy a mid morning boost too, mind if I join you?"
"Of course not, that'd be great!"

A few seconds later, the café owner opened the gate for us and we eagerly placed our orders for tea and pasties. Daniel told me more about his wife and children. It was a treat to see him talk about them, I could tell he adored the ground they walked on, and I felt a great sense of appreciation to witness someone talk about their loved ones so proudly. After our tea break, we carried on walking a few miles together, spurring each other on through the summer heat. We passed lush farmland of ripening crops, rollercoaster sections of cliff tops and sweeping, crashing waves below. We passed a tiny little hamlet and got our hopes up for another refreshment as we saw a sign saying "Little Daisy café this way", but was sorely disappointed when we found out it had closed down.

Eventually we made it to Porthluney Cove. I was feeling pretty exhausted by that point and rejoiced when I saw a beach bar-café that we could stop at. It was a very cool looking place, almost tropical looking with rattan walls, canvas ceiling and acoustic music stage to the left. We had another fill of tea and pasties and our grumbling stomachs greedily soaked up the sustenance.

"Whereabouts are you camping tonight, Daniel?"

"There's quite a few sites around here to choose from so I think I'll carry on a few more miles to one of the furthest ones away. That way I can have an easier day tomorrow."

"Good idea, I think I'm done for the day now though! There's a campsite just up the road from here I think I'll have a go at." I said, food coma starting to sink in after the enormous amount of pastry I'd just consumed.

Daniel and I said our "see-you-soons" to each other and made our weary way to our campsites. I began to walk up the road to a place called Treveor Farm Campsite, about a mile away. Of course there had to be one final massive hill to climb before I got there. Finally, after puffing and panting and groaning my way up the hill, I staggered into the campsite entrance. There was a blonde lady in her 30s wearing well-worn dungarees tending to the garden, who I assumed must've been the owner. She welcomed me with the biggest, sweetest smile and words of encouragement as she guessed correctly what I was doing. I told her highlights of my journey so far and why I was doing it.

"Oh, love, I'm totally in awe of you honestly! Here, this one's on me, you can stay here for free tonight. You deserve it!" she said with a warmth that filled my heart.

"Really? Oh my goodness, thank you so so much, that really means so much to me!" I said with tears in my eyes. Once again I was humbled and blown away by the generosity of my fellow human beings.

I set up camp, hopped over to the shower block to soak my sun-worn skin, legs close to collapse after a tough 12 mile hike and finally crawled into my tent as the cooler evening began to set in. Contentedness washed over me at another day completed on this path and I soon fell asleep, the mooing cows in the next field singing me a lullaby.

Day 34. I woke to the ripe smell of a working farm beginning its chores for the day. Maybe it's the country girl in me, but there's something I find utterly delicious and comforting about the smell of fertiliser and manure.
"Fresh country air! Nothing like it!" as my Mum always says. She's right. Tractors began rumbling their engines for another day of ploughing, cows and sheep moo-ed and baa-ed to each other. And the campers around me slurping first coffees and first teas in preparation for another day of British summer. My morning routine passed quickly, efficiently and simply and I set off eagerly back down the road to rejoin my beloved path. My home.

The weather today was cloudy and really muggy, feeling like there was a storm on the horizon. The electricity in the air made my sunkissed unruly hair go all fluffy. My end destination for

today was 12 miles away, a place called
Charlestown near the famous brewery town of St
Austell but today was another strenuous section
of the SWCP and at times I huffed and puffed
and wailed out loud, "Ugggggh I thought the
south side was meant to be easier!!"

For some reason, this section I was walking
today seemed to have an infinite number of
flights of steps. More than any other day
previously. Giant slabs of slate mixed with rickety
wooden and dirt ledges, some flights seemed to
go on forever, and sometimes they were so
steep I had to use my hands and feet to climb up
them like a ladder. I'd do a little celebratory jig
everytime I reached the top of one flight of
steps. Only to despair again when I had to go
back down the other side of a valley and then up
the next one.

Up and down, up and down, up and down I
hoisted and heaved myself and my pack over
the terrain, passing dainty fishing villages along
the way, but not particularly paying much
attention to them. The pain in my left foot was
starting to return.
"No. No, India. You will NOT get injured again.
Not this time." I said sternly to myself, brow
furrowed, eyes fixed firmly to another flight of
steps I was traversing. Mum was spending the
weekend exploring in her little motorhome as
she did every weekend and was meeting me at
Charlestown at the end of the day. I was a couple

miles away from her and the thought of having a restock spurred me on. Stomach grumbling as always for something carb loaded and filling.

I met up with Mum at a local pub in Charlestown that had a garden that they'd let us camp in overnight. We had a huge pub dinner there and my eyes were soon drooping from a full day of physicality and a full belly. Snuggled up in my tent, light rain began falling as I massaged my feet out. My left foot was feeling tender so I made sure to take good care of it and promised myself half a day's rest tomorrow.

Day 35. Charlestown to Par. Three miles. That's it. That's all I could do today. I haven't had a rest day for two weeks and my left foot is feeling it. So I did the easy and flat walk from Charlestown, past Carlyon Bay and around to Par in an hour and a half today. I said goodbye to Mum this morning as she continued her weekend of exploring and I set up camp at Penhale Farm Campsite. I pitched my spot a few feet away from the toilets and showers so I didn't have to walk far and spent the rest of the day watching fluffy clouds float by a calm blue sky.

Eventually the white clouds began to turn mottled shades of pink and then fiery oranges and reds and all of a sudden, the sky was lit on fire by the setting sun. It was so breathtakingly beautiful I cried at the sight of it. That's one of the things I love about sunsets: you never see the same sunset twice. Every cloud casts a different light, the seasons change and so do the colours with it. I mused, once again as I often did when I watched the sunset about my journey so far. The path may not be getting easier... but I was certainly getting stronger... I thought to myself. And isn't that a metaphor for life?

Day 36. I woke up, did my morning routine and went to put my walking boots on. Ew... The past almost six weeks of continuous hiking, on my feet all day everyday in all weathers had taken a toll on my poor little boots. I hadn't realised before, but the soles were coming away quite a bit from the now-no-so-waterproof fabric uppers. And the fabric of the boots themselves had holes all over them.

"Ahh, that's why my feet have been so wet these past couple days!" I chuckled to myself. All the groundwater from the morning dew collecting on the foliage beside the path was consistently running into my boots and my feet had felt continuously damp for the past week.

I squelched along the coast path, grimacing with discomfort at the warm odorous liquid pooling in my boots beneath the soles of my feet.

"Gnnnnn... ok... well, I guess the time has come to get a new pair." I said to myself as I wandered into the picturesque seaside village of Fowey. There in the distance stood a beacon of light - praise be, a Mountain Warehouse! I entered the tiny store and instantly began accidentally knocking camping gear, enamel mugs and lines of thermal socks over with the massive load on my back like a bull in a china shop.

"Oops, oh gosh, so sorry, oops, just need to... squeeze through... excuse me..." I muttered to a disgruntled tourist buying sandals for her young child.

"Good morning! How are you doing? Would you like any help at all?" said the friendly young chap behind the till.

"Hi! Yes, I just need to buy some new boots, I've worn through this pair." I said, gesturing to my boots which seemed to have aged significantly more as I stood beside the display of shiny clean new ones.

"Hello! Hey you look like you could be an ambassador for us, I recognise everything you're wearing!" said the other equally lovely assistant as she beamed an approving smile at my Mountain Warehouse outfit.

"Haha, yes, feel free to sponsor me, that would be great." I winked at her only half joking.

The two shop assistants proceeded to help me pick out a replacement pair of boots and excitedly fussed around me, genuinely taking care in making sure I got the right ones as I told them about my journey. Eventually, I found a pair that felt just right, walked out wearing them, waved a cheerful goodbye to the Mountain Warehouse staff and stood outside on the street by a waste bin, my arms cradling my old tatty boots.

A wave of emotion washed over me as I held my old brown-grey boots in my arms.
"Well. Farewell old friends. Thank you for carrying me these past 400 miles. It is time for your ceremonial burial. Wish me luck for the rest of the journey." I said with a tear in my eye as I opened the chewing-gum-and-cigarette-butt-decorated waste bin and gently placed the boots inside. I laughed out loud at the fact that I was crying at throwing away a pair of shoes. People passing by looked at me in puzzlement. I was used to that by now.

I carried on with the path, feeling light as a feather with a huge spring in my step in my shiny new footwear as I realised how much the previous pair of boots was slowing me down. This new pair coordinated with my red patterned leggings and navy fleece, they were navy with red side sections and red laces. I felt very hip and very much like something out of a hiking catalogue.

From Fowey, I caught the little ferry across the river to Polruan, then from there it was a strenuous walk up and down numerous cliffs and valleys with yet more flights of steep steps. I steamed up and down them though with renewed vigour. The cliff faces were stunning in this area. Dark slate and dramatically sheer with the rolling ocean waves below. By the time I got to Polperro though, after a long 13 mile day, I was exhausted.

Polperro is the town that you see on all the Cornish postcards. Very much a tourist hotspot, and I looked around at the narrow cobbled streets, the dainty cottages, indie shops and tiny little fishing harbour and couldn't help but be swept up in the charm of it all. I think I even cooed out loud at how gosh-darn pretty it is. But the rain was rumbling in, and I was eager to do one final push up one final massive hill to Great Kellow Farm Campsite a mile inland and set up camp for the day. It was a struggle. Back bent forward 45 degrees, arms swinging by my side, propelling me forward with my walking poles, squinting, grumbling, panting my way up the steep tarmac road as fat rain droplets began splashing against my hot face.

At last, I made it to the campsite, checked in with the farmer's wife who ran it and raced to pitch my tent next to the shower block just before a torrential storm arrived. I sat, a little damp and cold, in my tent but cosy enough wrapped up in my sleeping bag. I decided that eating cold rations in my tent tonight was just not an option so I gathered my cooking things together to prepare a hot meal inside the shower block. It was a little after 5pm and just as I was hunched over in my tent trying to put my raincoat back on as the rain thundered outside, I heard the frustrated cries of a couple trying to set up camp in this weather. They sounded well spoken with lovely home-county-middle-class accents.

"Oh, Nigel!! What are we going to do, everything is so wet!"

"Come on Catherine sweetheart, it'll be ok, look here let's shelter in the shower block and wait it out for a while."

My newly arrived campmates sounded in despair so I gathered my cooking supplies and dashed into the shower block to introduce myself and see if I could be of assistance. I walked in and saw a bedraggled middle-aged couple with kind faces shaking off waterproofs and hiking kit and groaning at the bad luck they'd just had.

"Hi there! Are you guys ok? Can I give you a hand with anything? Ooh are you hiking the coast path?" I asked.

"Oh hello there, pleased to meet you, we're ok now we're sheltered in here. Just need to get all this blasted kit dry... but yes we are hiking the coast path, all of it in fact, though I'm struggling to remember why we decided to do this bahaha... how about you? Are you on your own?" chuckled Nigel as Catherine was firing up their camping stove behind him.

"Ah amazing! Yes I'm hiking the entire coast path in one go as well! And yes I am on my own. Rotten weather out there, hey?" I said setting up my own cooking supplies on the opposite side of the shower block.

Catherine, Nigel and I introduced ourselves to each other properly and then got down to the compulsory nitty gritty of comparing our journeys so far along this sacred path as we prepared our own dinners. They told me that they were a married couple from Bournemouth and had always wanted to hike the coast path. They told me how it essentially felt like a really long walk home as they would end their walk when they reached Bournemouth which was a little further along than the official end point of Poole. They had a kind and generous spirit and offered me a hot cup of tea and a slice of cake. "Oh thank you so much! But... I feel I should be offering YOU something as you came here in such a state! I don't have anything though haha..." I said gratefully accepting the tea and small round sweet eccles cake.
"Not a worry at all - we are happy to share and take care of our fellow hiker!" Catherine said as she used the hand dryer to blast her wet fleece with warm air.

We carried on getting to know each other well into the evening until the sky was getting darker and darker. The rain still did not cease when we said goodnight and quickly army-crawled into our tents. The heavy rain sounded soothing on my little canvas roof. It was very windy as well, but my little shelter, so close to the ground and

so small, held up just fine. Tomorrow I will begin
the sixth week of my epic adventure, I mused to
myself. I couldn't wait to see what it brought.

Week 6 – Humdrum & Humble

Day 37. I woke up at the same time as my new
friends Catherine and Nigel. The storm had
raged overnight but I'd had a cosy night's sleep
in my tent that sat so close to the ground that
the wind that howled overnight seemed to glide
right over me. This morning the air had that
clean, renewed scent that always comes after a
storm and the sun was just beginning to peek
through the lighter desaturated clouds.

The three of us ate our breakfasts together and
pondered about the upcoming route today. The
guidebook promised an easier day, Polperro to
Portwrinkle with Looe in between, over rambling
cliffs and dainty port towns and we decided to
walk the day together.
"Hey, let's all get a taxi back down the hill to
Polperro this morning, save our legs a little bit!"
Catherine said.
"Ooh good idea!" I replied gratefully.

We arrived back down in Polperro after a short
but much needed taxi ride and got a quick cup
of tea at one of the little cafés there. Then we
began our walk for the day. Catherine, Nigel and
I got a good pace going up into the gentle cliffs
of the South Cornwall coast, the sun shone
brighter and brighter throughout the morning
and my heart filled with love for this couple that
were quickly feeling like my trail-parents. We

talked non-stop about our lives, our loves, our losses, as our feet fell into rhythm on the wonderful path we were now sharing.

I often silently wondered at all the amazing people I'd met on my journey so far. Each one a little wacky, each one with a fascinating story to tell, each one a kindred spirit and Nigel and Catherine were no exceptions. They were a little bit bonkers, bags of personality and just down to earth, kind hearted, genuinely good people.

We reached Looe, eight miles later, by lunchtime and we were all starving. Diving into the nearest pasty shop, the ecstatic aroma of warm pastry and hot tea filled my nostrils and sent my stomach into ravenous overdrive. Nigel bought the three of us pasties and lattés which I tried and failed to insist on paying for mine.
"No no, India, I insist, I'd like to get these. Catherine and I are grateful for your companionship today! You are really helping to spur us on!" Nigel said.

We ate our lunch by the water side on the little seafront promenade at Looe, fiercely shielding our precious sustenance from the swirling sea birds above.
"Where are you stopping today, India? Our next campsite's only a couple miles away now, although we do feel we could carry on a bit further... but we thought we'd make the most of a shorter day and rest up a bit!" Catherine said.

"Well I'd hoped to carry on another six or seven miles to Portwrinkle and find somewhere to camp there. There's no campsite but I thought I'd ask around any pubs or cafés or something…" I trailed off, a hint of uncertainty creeping into my voice about where I'd sleep tonight.
"Really?! We don't want you wild-camping on your own! Are you sure you'll be ok?!"
"Haha guys don't worry. I'll be fine! I'll find somewhere. I'll text you when I'm safe. Promise." I replied a little too jovially.

I said an affectionate goodbye to my trail-parents and carried on walking the rest of the day on my own. The path was more strenuous from Looe with deeper valleys and taller cliffs which had me huffing and puffing in the early afternoon sun. Some dramatic clouds still lingered above the ocean in a crescent shape as if a raging dragon had stormed through the land overnight and was now calmly carrying on his voyage out to the calm blue sea. He has said all that he needed to and now left a warm fairweather atmosphere in his wake.

Finally, after passing through Seaton, then Downderry, staggering and exhausted as usual, I made it to Portwrinkle. It was a tiny little village on the cliff tops that didn't have as many camping possibilities as I thought it might. There was a cliff edge car park with the odd grassy patch just big enough to pitch my tent on… but a massive sign stating "STRICTLY NO

CAMPING". There were some public toilets which I even considered sleeping in... but the stench of old piss and cigarettes quickly made my mind up on that one. A golf club sprawled a little further on with neatly clipped grass, just perfect for me, but there were too many golfers with their starched checked trousers and knitted vests that I imagined I'd quickly be discovered and ushered on. There was one café though, with a promising looking garden and I eagerly gravitated towards it, my hopes of a safe space to sleep tonight rising.

Entering the café, I bought myself a cup of hot tea, both for my spirits and as a way to trade my boarding for the night. I floated the idea to the two ladies behind the counter.
"Oh we'd love to help you out, really, but our owner is pretty strict on these things. We've had it before, SWCP hikers wanting to camp here, but we just can't allow it, I'm so sorry..." one of the ladies said genuinely.
I sat down anyway in the café and enjoyed my cup of tea, but feeling a little self-conscious now at the rapidly advancing day and the prospect of where I'd sleep tonight. A grandmother and her young granddaughter entered the café, ordered hot drinks and cakes and sat down on the table next to me. We chit-chatted politely to each other, just small talk about the weather, what we were each doing today and I considered in my mind asking if I could stay with them tonight before the grandmother mentioned that they

had a long drive home shortly which put that thought out the window.

Finishing my cup of tea, I wandered back outside again, dithering and looking around to see if I'd missed anywhere suitable. A rough-looking drunk man, dribbling with no teeth, suspicious staines on his clothes and pupils the size of tennis balls slumped on the park bench next to where I stood and mumbled at me. I couldn't decipher what he was saying to me but the way he was looking me up and down made my skin crawl.

Oh god, oh god, oh god I really have to find somewhere now! I squealed internally to myself. I quickly started walking back down the road, away from the creepy drunk guy, when I saw something that made my spirits soar and tears well in my eyes. Was it a mirage? Was it real? Surely... It must be...

"INDIAAA!! Oh we're so happy we found you! After you left we decided we just couldn't let you wild-camp on your own so we pushed on walking and now we're here and we found you! Oh thank goodness!" Catherine cheered as the words spilled from her mouth in an excited rush. "Catherine!! Nigel!! I can't believe you're here! Oh I'm so relieved too, I've just been wandering around for the past hour trying to figure out where I'm going to sleep but I haven't found anywhere yet." I said embracing my people with tears in my eyes.

"Well here's the plan: we are going to get a taxi back to our campsite just outside of Looe where we'd originally planned to stay and you'll stay there with us and then tomorrow morning we can get another taxi back here and carry on where we left off, ok?" Nigel said in his best protective-Dad-man-with-a-plan-voice.

"Yes. Amazing. I'm so grateful. Honestly, thank you so much."

And so, happily reunited, our little trail family got a taxi back to Bay View Campsite. A farm campsite in the hills above Looe with a flowery homey bungalow in the middle lived in by the lady who runs it. And she was a trail angel for sure. Catherine, Nigel and I rocked up with all our gear, sweaty and tired and checked in with our trail angel. She was super enthusiastic about what we were doing and the reasons why. So much so that she let us stay there for free with the promise that we'd put the campsite fees into our donations for our charities.

We contentedly set up camp for the night and it wasn't long before we were all cozied up in our tents after a quick camp-stove meal. Hearts full. Bellies not quite full but satisfied enough. Souls fulfilled with the human connection, human kindness and abundance of human generosity in the world. Rain began to fall again, but just ever so lightly.

"Goodnight, India." "Goodnight, Catherine."
Goodnight, Nigel."

Day 38. Today has been a joyous day. One I will
never forget. But more on that later. Catherine,
Nigel and I woke up early, sped through the
morning routine and got a taxi back down to
Portwrinkle, eager to get started on the trail in
which we'd reach an important milestone 15
miles later. We started off walking again
together but they got into a slightly quicker
pace than me and we said our
"see-you-down-the-path" and separated into our
own journeys once more.

Today's a big one for me. Today I will reach
Plymouth. The gateway to my home area of
South Devon. I relished every last step of Cornish
soil as I fell into a steady rambling rhythm
around the Rame Peninsula. As I write this now, I
look back on this day with extra fondness and
with a tear in my eye. The young woman who
was walking the Cornish SWCP that day had no
idea that this small section of the path, just a
handful of months later, when autumn gently
whispered through the changing colours in the
trees, would begin to be her home. She had
fallen in love with Cornwall being on this path...
and she would soon fall in love with it again. Just
two months later. With a beautiful man who
lives in this very section. Day 38 - she'd be
walking right past where he lives. And she'd

have no idea of the beautiful adventure that waits for her just around the corner.

But back to the path, I had a very surreal feeling in my heart. Surreal in the sense that my home area was so close, yet I still had such a long way to go on this journey. I still had two large counties to walk through. The path today was extremely pretty. Back through the golf course I'd considered camping in yesterday, then onto a military firing range, the breathtaking sweep of Whitsand Bay and around the rugged cliff tops of Rame Head. Then from there, I walked around to the quaint villages of Kingsand and Cawsand and cheered in delight as I saw the sprawling urban landscape of Plymouth across the river. A final stunning woodland walk through the Mount Edgcumbe estate led me to the little Cremyll passenger ferry. I eagerly hopped onto it, my heart hammering in my chest at finally walking home. My heart was hammering for another reason as well. For the past couple days, I'd been in contact with my sisterhood. My dear friends had agreed to meet me in Plymouth to welcome me home and as I sat on the ferry, my body fizzed with excited energy. My brain whirred with questions at having been on my own and apart from them for the past six weeks. Will I look different to them? Will they look different? Will I seem like a different person? Has much happened since I've been gone?

The sisterhood I mention here are the incredible women I'd met when, in the 12 weeks prior to beginning my walk I approached a new friend of mine called Bella who had recently become a life coach and I'd enrolled in her new Empowered Goddess life coaching program. It was honestly the best investment I have ever made and I am so grateful for everything I learned and that she came into my life. She is a dear friend now. It certainly felt like the universe was gifting me exactly what I needed at exactly the right time. It was so transformative and I had a huge awakening.

With her counselling, suddenly my life made sense. I discovered where my saviour-complex came from, my need to be the giver, the fixer - from being a JW and being taught that women were inferior, only created to serve men. I discovered how toxic lessons from my religious upbringing attracted my toxic relationship. Everything that had happened, I realised, wasn't my fault but it was my responsibility to heal my inner wounds so that these damaging patterns and generational traumas stop happening. It was my responsibility to live as my authentic self and not live in my fearful shadow so I can create a better life for my future children, and their children.

I discovered that I had a deep limiting belief around failure which had been holding me back all my life but Bella's program empowered me to fall fiercely in love with myself. Self love really is the most important love and I learnt to accept all parts of myself. To forgive myself for the years of pain, lies and self-doubt.

There were of course painful breakthroughs along the way of those 12 weeks. When life gives you a lesson like what I'd been through over the past few years, it has to break you in order to put yourself back together again. Emotions that I'd never felt before came flooding out. All those years of burying my feelings, putting on a brave face, keeping the secrets of my relationship hidden. I could finally release them all. It was both wonderful and harrowing to acknowledge and lean into my grief.

We practised breathwork, meditation, conscious movement, talking therapy, inner child healing and the best part of all were the group coaching sessions with the other women on the program. I'd finally found community with these women as we held each other through each one's healing.

I realised that everything happens FOR us in life, not TO us. Every awakened person has gone through this process of complete breakage, but then put themselves back together again, learnt the lessons their soul was meant to learn, and finally rose back up like a Phoenix into their highest self. I wasn't ready to forgive *him*, but that's ok. It had only been four months at that point since I left my ex, the hurt was still raw, but now I had a much better perspective on everything and could really look back and feel actually grateful for the lessons learned and the fact that it had brought me to the awakening journey I was on now.

I couldn't believe how I didn't know any of this transformational magic before - it all made so much sense and felt so natural. I think deep down I've always known the radiant woman within, but the patriarchal society we live in seeks to suppress her. I revelled in self pleasure, self care and learnt (or could it be remembered?) so much about the soul, spirituality, chakras, Ayurveda, divine feminine and divine masculine energies. I devoured books such as Pussy by Regena Thomashauer, The Secret by Rhonda Byrne, Braving the Wilderness by Brené Brown, Untamed by Glenon Doyle and Eat, Feel, Fresh by Sahara Rose. Why aren't these valuable life skills taught in schools, I wondered? There is a chronic imbalance of the wounded masculine in our world. In order for our beautiful planet and all that inhabits her to heal, we must all turn to the divine feminine.

Back to the path, the ferry reached the other side of the river. Devon! I was home! I hopped off the boat, raced around the old military stone buildings of Royal William Yard and started walking up onto Plymouth Hoe.

"EEEEEEEEEK!!!"
"AAAAAAAAAAAAH!!!"
"INDIAAAAAA!!!"
"HEYYYY GUYS!!!"

I saw Beth first. In her lovely signature sunflower dungarees. I started crying. We ran up to each other and gave each other the biggest hug. Then I saw Aimée, in her glorious flared trousers, long silky black hair and hippie jewellery, and she joined in the pile of hugs. Onlookers watched with amused smiles as we tearfully embraced and started talking about a million things we had to catch up on. Bella came into view. My dear friend and coach who had helped me so much. I cried more as we wrapped our arms around each other.
The four of us sat down at a pizza place by the waterside and I eagerly waited for the last person to arrive.

And there she was. My sister. Betsy. Racing down the steps towards me with her fiancé Connor and their dog Rafi in tow. I ran to her and we tearfully hugged for the longest time.
"You're so tanned, I can't believe it!! You're more tanned than me!!" she said laughing. This was a recurring joke between us. Betsy has Italian heritage with long brunette hair, olive skin and deep brown eyes, and me the quintessential fair, freckly, auburn english rose. We'd always laugh about how she'd get super tanned in the

summer and I'd stay super pale, but with a few more freckles.

I gave a big bear hug to Connor as well who had been like another brother to me these past few years. We all spent the rest of the evening joyfully catching up with each other, eating pizza and drinking wine. I only had one small glass and that was enough to get me tipsy, so accustomed was I to not having a drop of alcohol now. I regaled my friends with my adventures so far and it felt so good to share all that I had learnt and all that I had realised about myself. And I still had two more weeks left of walking. The journey was not yet over.

At the end of the night, my stomach satisfied with pizza, I went back to Betsy's place to stay for the night. She lived just a short ten minute drive away through the city centre and I couldn't wait to rest my head down on a proper pillow and a proper mattress for the night. As soon as we walked through her front door she got to cooking me up a quick vegetable stir fry.
"India you've lost weight, you need to get these veggies in you! You can't survive off those bloody military packs!" she said affectionately.
She marvelled at how much I had eaten this evening. A whole massive pizza and a large veggie stir fry. My stomach felt like it would pop. My eyes soon became droopy as the onset of a food coma quickly settled into my body.

I took full advantage of her washing machine and threw my one set of filthy clothes in, borrowing some of her sweatpants and t-shirt to wear for the rest of the evening after a hot shower.. As soon as my head hit the pillow of the bed in Betsy's spare bedroom, I was out for the count. My tired body breathing a sweet sight of relief at something squishy to rest on after a long 15 mile hike.

After my high of finally reaching Devon, the next few days passed by in a familiar, regular, almost mundane blur of coast path that I knew like the back of my hand. Day 39: Plymouth to Newton Ferrers. 12 miles. Day 40: Newton Ferrers to Bigbury. Another 12 miles. Day 41: Bigbury to Salcombe. Another 12 miles. Day 42: Salcombe to Slapton 16 miles. Day 43: Slapton to Kingswear. Another 12 miles.

It was a wet five days with consistent warm rain that soaked me and my kit through. I couldn't get anything dry and morale began to dip as mould crept through my tent. My own stench souring with days old moisture that made me gag with every movement spoiling the fresher air around me. On the morning of day 41, I'd discovered I'd made a grave error overnight. I thought it would've been a good idea to leave my boots in the tiny porch area between the inner and outer layers of my tent to dry out overnight. Big mistake. It had rained heavily whilst I slept and the rain had filled my boots to the brim with dish-water-brown liquid. I'd spent a frantic 15 minutes trying desperately to squeeze the water out from my boots and dry them with my pathetic microfibre towel. But to no avail. I squelched through the miles monotonously. This section of the walk was probably the easiest physically. But definitely the hardest mentally. I ramped up my motivational self-speeches. The sun WILL return. I WILL get dry. I WILL feel clean soon. One day, I WILL smell good again!

One thing that really helped morale was meeting another beautiful soul. On day 42, I met a wonderful man in his 60s called David. He was a Magistrate and had come to hike the South Devon section of the coast path. He'd been completing hiking the SWCP in sections over a number of years and the South Devon section was his last to complete. He was such a gentle, kind and interesting man and we shared many deep conversations as we walked together that day and whilst bumping into each other over the following days. I was grateful for his companionship that really helped to spur me on in those damp days.

Another morale boost was on Day 43. Passing through the busy town of Dartmouth, I'd met up with two of my Fifty5a customers who had become more like friends over the years. Two sisters called Monica and Helena. We had hot drinks and slices of cake together at a café there and they were so sweet in offering me words of encouragement.

That evening in my mouldy smelly tent, surrounded by my mouldy smelly possessions, as the rain gently pitter-pattered on my canvas roof, a wave of gratitude washed over me. I smiled to myself and felt so thankful to be here. Despite the current physical discomfort I was in, I felt so grateful that I had been able to press the reset button on my life. The past few years had been so painful, but this path, this beautiful journey, has healed me so deeply, so profoundly. I feel as though I've had a complete cleanse of my mind, body and soul.

I fell asleep to the sound of the rain and the smell of my own filthy stench. A wide grin spread across my lips in contentment.

Week 7 – Up & Up

Day 44. Week seven! I couldn't believe how quickly these weeks had passed. But at the same time, it strangely felt as though I'd been on this path forever. I never wanted it to end. And today, JOY of all JOYS! The weather was warm and dry! It was a stunning walk through steep wooded valleys and the high red cliffs of South Devon. I passed an old WW2 bunker and walked for a couple of miles with three beautiful stallion horses that I chatted outloud to. They were curious, handsome fellows that walked beside me as so many other new friends had on my journey so far. They gave me gentle nudges of encouragement on my shoulders with their soft velvet noses and I thought to myself that they were probably the most special friends I'd made on my path so far.

Today was another exciting day. I'd just walked 11 miles to the busy fishing hub of Brixham and waited in the main car park there. And a few feet in the distance a beautiful feisty blonde Swedish lady, jumping up and down, enthusiastically waved at me from her car. It was Malin, my former boss at Fifty5a, mentor and almost surrogate mother for the past nine years. We ran up to each other and had a big hug.
"India, you look so tanned!"
"Haha lots of people have been saying that to me recently!" I chuckled with a wry smile.

Malin took me back to her house in Totnes
where Aron, husband and business partner, and
my former colleague Sophie were waiting. We
were getting the band back together for one
night only and Malin was cooking us a delicious
dinner. I had a lovely long shower in their
bathroom and Malin had prepared chicken with
numerous side salads, an abundance of fresh
food that I gorged on. They kept refilling my
plate as she happily exclaimed, "India, I've never
seen you eat so much! Where does it go?!
There's nothing of you!"
We spent the evening catching up, them asking
me a bunch of questions about my journey so
far and me eagerly telling them every detail.

After dinner, Malin took me back home to Dad's
place where I'd be staying for the next couple
nights. It was so good to see my dear family
again after weeks apart, giving them long
cuddles and kisses. My kit and myself were
growing more mouldy by the day and were in
desperate need of cleaning and airing out now
the weather had improved. Tomorrow, I will head
back up to North Devon to do the bit around
Hartland Quay that I skipped as I'd already done
the Brixham to Babbacombe section after my
injury that would've been tomorrow's route. I felt
content at the prospect of tying up loose ends.

Day 45. Dad and I drove directly north, back up
to Hartland Quay to do the supposedly severe six

miles that I'd skipped all the way back on day nine. It felt strange coming back. My heart swelled with love and familiarity. Like coming home. The prodigal daughter returns to the path that once would've broken her. But this time she's stronger. Her leg muscles are toned and twice as big now. Her core muscles rippled with strength to power through the sheer valleys and cliffs abundant in this area.

The first four miles of this section was easy breezy, high on the black cliff tops of North Devon and I got almost cocky.
"Pah, this isn't severe at all! Don't know what the guidebook's talking about, where are all these steep valleys?!" I exclaimed out loud.

And then it came. Of course, my beloved path never fails to humble me. She's a tough mistress. I'd reached Welcombe Mouth, three miles from my finish line of Morwenstow and THAT is when the severe valleys started. FIVE of them crammed into three miles! Up and down, up and down, up and down, an exhilarating roller coaster that in week two would've ruined me. But now, I powered through them with all the expertise of a seasoned thru-hiker.

I saw Dad waiting for me at the top of the final valley looking down at me with his binoculars, waving enthusiastically. I waved back and powered on up to him.

"Hey Ind, you made it in record time! How was that my darling? You don't look too tired?"
"Phew! That was pretty wild! I feel great though! I feel like I could do that all again!" I said honestly. And it was true. I felt super proud of myself and super exhilarated. So that was that. Loose ends tied up. Now it was just the final week and a half left until I finished completely. My heart ached with an emotion I couldn't quite yet put into words.

Day 46. Back down to Babbacombe in South Devon. My kit was now clean and dry after spending the past 18 hours drying out. I was feeling ready and raring to go. Today was going to be another short day, just six and a half miles, as I would literally be walking home to the little village called Combeinteignhead, two miles inland from Shaldon, where Mum and I rented our flat. I was so looking forward to it. As I rambled through the clifftop woods, shaded from the sweltering summer heat, through a section of the SWCP I knew so well, I fantasised about what I would do tonight. I mentally planned a whole pamper evening for myself. The weather was hot, hot, hot and I sweated buckets, feeling even more grateful at the promise of a deep cleanse tonight. The path swept and curved up and down and around the brick-red cliffs and lush woodland until eventually leading out to the little village of Shaldon. Then, I diverted off the coast path and began to walk the Templer Way path inland along the estuary.

It's an old granite mining route, 18 miles long,
that links Haytor on Dartmoor to Teignmouth
and Shaldon.

I love this walk. Over the past few months I'd
spent many days stomping up and down this
estuary, contemplating life, dreaming of the
future and all the hopes and plans I held about
it. It felt like a full-circle moment to be walking
back along it whilst fulfilling one of the dreams
I'd fantasised about on these very pebbles. It
really is a beautiful part of the world. Like a scene
from a Studio Ghibli movie, it's all rolling hills,
lush green farmland, gently lapping water and
train tracks on the other side of the river that
supported many passengers travelling from
Newton Abbot to Teignmouth and beyond.

And then, I stood outside the front door to my
flat, in the little village I'd recently come to call
home. A curious emotion bubbled up inside me.
I almost didn't want to be here. Of course, I was
looking forward to spending one night in my
own bed... or was I? The pull of the wild called
me back. My green sausage sleeping bag, my
tiny khaki tent, spending all day everyday in the
womb of Mother Earth. That. That is home.

But I was also in dire need of a shower and my
washing machine. Mum and I gave each other
the biggest hug and I got down to filling her in
on all the things that had happened since I last
saw her. We spent the early evening catching up,

having dinner together, and then after dinner I took myself off for my pamper session.

I ran a hot bubble bath, candles, incense, a cup of herbal tea, the works. As I lay naked in the delicious aromatic water, I examined how my body had changed these past seven weeks. My hands had become calloused and rough from gripping the walking poles. My stomach had ripples of abs I never knew existed. My butt was firm where it once had been soft and jiggly. My legs had seen the biggest transformation. No longer were they slim sticks. My thighs and calves were big steaks of toned muscle, firm and strong, well-oiled hiking machines, with an abundance of thick hair from having not shaved for all this time. My skin had patches of a rich tan from the parts of me that had been exposed to the sun, my face a constellation of freckles.

I looked at myself for a long time. And what I saw was love. Love in its purest, most beautiful form.

I emerged from my bath, legs and armpits shaved, hair washed and conditioned, moisturised my skin and I felt completely reborn. I was floating on a cloud of relaxation as I slipped into my own bed, my own soft cotton sheets, and slipped into the most blissful deep sleep I've ever had.

Day 47. I practically leapt out of my bed early in the morning, eager to get back to my beloved path. If all is well, I was on track to finish completely in nine days time. I wanted to relish every last day, every moment of this final stretch of my journey. After breakfast, I said goodbye to Mum.

"Well, my darling! The next time I see you will be at the finish line!" she said with a tear in her eye.

"Eek, I know! I love you, Mum. I know I've said it before but I really do appreciate all the support you've given me on this journey." I replied, giving her a big squeeze.

It was another super hot day as I made my way back down the estuary and across the river to Teignmouth. My backpack felt newly heavier after restocking supplies at my flat and I quickly began to sweat. The 12 mile route today was easy and flat along the seawall between Teignmouth and Dawlish, around the nature reserve and tourist park at Dawlish Warren and then to Starcross to get the ferry across the Exe estuary to Exmouth, although the heat made it much more challenging than normal.

It's a route I know and love and have done a thousand times before. Towards the end of the seawall at Teignmouth, there's a rock that protrudes out of the ocean, proudly erect, that looks remarkably phallic-like and I said my usual, "Hello, Willy Rock!" as I had done many times before, giggling to myself. The ocean was so exquisitely beautiful today, it took my breath away at various points. I couldn't remember the last time I'd seen it so blue and sparkly before.

Once I reached Exmouth, I set up camp on the seafront on the green space where all the motorhomes park up and settled in for the evening. Tomorrow, I will begin the long stretch along the Jurassic Coast. The final section. I flicked through my battered SWCP guidebook. From day one, I'd been ripping the pages out in an attempt to save weight in my backpack and it was now becoming a crispy, washed out, weather beaten husk. I chuckled at all the memories these tatty pieces of paper held and promised to myself to keep the shell of it as a souvenir.

Day 48. I woke up to sub-saharan heat. Stifling air filled my nostrils, sapped the moisture from my eyes. Wow. I threw open the flaps to my tent and gasped for the fresh air, groping around for my water bottle as well. I'd slept naked and quickly decided that I would walk in just my leggings and bra today. No t-shirt, certainly no fleece. If it was legal I would've walked naked. But it was glorious. After all the rain the previous week, my heart leapt with joy and excitement at doing the final leg of this journey in this beautiful sunshine.

Coming out of Exmouth and passing the pointed obelisk that signifies the start of the Jurassic Coast, the path ambled through a large caravan park, then over many mid-sized red cliffs and farmland of ripening crops. I reached the little town of Budleigh Salterton which was buzzing with holiday makers and families enjoying a day at the beach. At the other end of the beach, the River Otter cut through the shingle too deeply for me to wade across without getting my kit completely soaked. I stood on the riverside, hands on my hips, pondering how to cross it when the family lounging next to me on their beach towels asked if I needed help.

"Are you alright there, love? Hey, my boy's just down there on his paddleboard, he can give you a lift across if you like!" said the mother.

"Oh that would be so helpful if he doesn't mind doing that, I'd be so grateful, thank you!"

And so proceeded perhaps one of my favourite memories on this path. A small but mighty act of kindness from a 12 year old boy who, once his mission was accomplished, visibly beamed with pride. The boy paddled up to me on his board, bristling at being deemed a hero and saving the day for a damsel in distress. I put my backpack on his board first and he paddled it across to the tiny beach on the other side of the river. Then he paddled back to me and I hopped on and he took me across to the other side. By this point a small crowd had gathered to watch the show and when the boy's mission was successfully completed and I was safely on the other side of the river, both me and my pack still dry and intact, we all erupted into applause, laughter and cheer for the joyful moment. The boy tried to play it cool but we could all see that he was giddy with pride. I bid farewell to those kind souls and carried on my way.

From Budleigh Salterton, the path became more challenging traversing steeper cliffs and deeper valleys and I dripped with sweat as the sun scorched in a cloudless azure sky. Salty water poured from my pores and ran down my skin almost faster than I could replenish it and it took a real conscious effort to keep drinking, keep hydrated. But I was thriving on it, my body was so fine tuned for hiking now that I could really just sit back, enjoy and feel fully present in my surroundings. I felt every inch the wild, sweaty goddess wonder-woman as I power walked to Sidmouth.

When I eventually did reach Sidmouth after a 13 mile hike, I was pretty knackered. There was a campsite I wanted to stay at high up in the hills behind the busy town that I just couldn't be bothered to walk to so I phoned a local taxi to take me there. After a short taxi ride, I checked in to Salcombe Regis campsite. A beautiful site nestled amongst rich woodland of oak, beech and spruce trees and I set up my little tent amongst the sheltered shade of one such large spruce. I cooled off in the showers, quickly heated up and ate one of my ration packs and fell asleep well before nightfall. Tomorrow is the last walk of the South Devon coast. The day after that: Dorset. Contentedness and satisfaction radiated throughout my body like the finest moisturiser to my soul.

Day 49. I woke up at the crack of dawn, 05:00am and made a resolution to myself to try and start walking everyday by 07:00am at the latest to do the majority of the hiking in the cooler mornings. That way I'd be done by early afternoon and then could spend the rest of the day relaxing, enjoying the sunshine and the sea.

Leaving Salcombe Regis Campsite, I walked through stunning woodland high up in the hills, using my map to guide me back to the coast path. I took a couple of wrong turns, but that didn't bother me, the area was so darn pretty. Eventually I found the right way, an overgrown path that I had to hack my way through before finally coming back out onto the coast path. And as I emerged through the foliage and onto the cliff tops at 07:30am, I burst into tears at the beauty I was feeling so privileged to witness. The sun was just rising to the East, glazing the world in a soft peach haze, and all was still and quiet. There was just a hint of faraway birdsong and a gentle lapping of waves far below. I took a moment to close my eyes, take some deep breaths and really soak it all up.

I was hiking again today in just my leggings and bra. Even this early in the morning the temperature was reaching mid-20s. I rolled up my t-shirt around my straps to add as extra padding as my skin was once again developing red friction burns from coming into such close direct sweaty contact with the pack straps.

The route today was hilly to say the least. But just so beautiful. I walked up and down cliffs that started out brick red, then turned into the white chalk that is synonymous with this area. The sea was crystal blue, matching the cloudless sky that sparkled sapphire. The plant life was lush and deep green. I weeped with happiness at various points along the walk. The beauty of it all was just overwhelming. I felt so grateful to witness it, to be in it, to BE it.

I stopped briefly halfway at Branscombe beach and couldn't resist having a quick dip in the glass-clear waters. I swam just in my underwear and dried off almost instantly in the heat of the day. After a quick tea stop at the café there and a warm conversation with a few of the locals, I carried on back up into the cliffs. There was a gentle salty sea breeze cruising in from the ocean that brushed my skin like a gentle lover's caress. As if the wind was giving me affectionate words of encouragement. The sun was shining bright yellow in the sky, the day could only be described as pleasant. Pleasant, content and deeply satisfying that just nourished me to my core.

The path gently began to amble down and down until reaching the popular beach town of Seaton. I power walked along the promenade, almost as a way of challenging myself further as a part of me felt like today was too easy, despite all the up and down cliff walking. I crossed the River Axe and made my way a little inland to the village of Axmouth and the riverside campsite there where I'd decided to stop for the day. The elderly couple that run the Axmouth Camping Site were so lovely and kind to me and let me stay for free. I thanked them profusely for their generosity and they showed me to my little spot by the green hedgerow with the river bank gently lapping behind. My camp neighbours were equally as friendly, an ex-car-salesman chap next to me called James was visiting his family whilst doing conservation work on the river as his new start-up business and a family opposite me in their motorhome with a great taste in music gently playing from their stereo.

I spent the rest of the day as I always did, massaging my feet and legs, taking it slow and easy, cooking my little military packs on my camp stove and cozying up in my sleeping bag reading my maps and guidebook. I'd read through my guidebook hundreds of times at this point, but the words never failed to soothe me as the evening drew in. Tomorrow was Monday. Exactly a week from now, if I stay on track, my beautiful adventure will come to an end. I had walked 530 miles. There was just 100 left to do.

"I don't want to stop. Not yet. I'm not ready." I
whispered to myself with tears in my eyes as the
moon and stars began blinking an expression of
unconditional love down upon the Earth.

Week 8 – Becoming

Day 50. Day. 50. D.A.Y. F.I.F.T.Y!! In some ways, my time on this wonderful path had gone so quickly, but I also felt that she and I had been as one for forever. Something within me had changed profoundly these past couple months. I had found it in the wilderness. And this morning, as I woke up in my tent to another day in beautiful hot summer sunshine, I had no idea that, in a couple of hours, that special something would be personified and stare me straight in the face...

Leaving Axmouth campsite, I started walking back down the river to rejoin the coast path. Today, according to the guidebook, will be one of pure remoteness through a nature reserve. Only one way in and one way out, my idea of heaven! I rejoined the coast path and climbed up onto some low cliffs with fields of wheat and corn. The fields were a beautiful shade of gold and the crops swayed a gentle rumba in the ease of the morning's slowness.

Then the coast path came to a dark tunnel of hedgerow. The day was so bright, but here in this tunnel was the faintest scarcity of light. My heart fluttered. It's time for Alice to go down the rabbit hole. Down we go. A sign saying "Welcome to the Axmouth to Lyme Regis Undercliffs Nature Reserve" stated a little bit of history about the place. Over many centuries, long ago, a series of cliff falls took place in this area causing it to become inaccessible for human habitation. Thus, nature took over, totally reclaimed the land and now it is five long miles of virtually untouched densely thick jungle paradise for wildlife and plantlife alike. The only sign of human activity is the coast path winding its way through. Just one path. Only one way in, one way through, and one way out. I squealed with excitement and stepped into the abyss.

One mile in. I've gasped several times in awe. My head swivelled frantically this way and that, my eyes trying with all their might to take in the amount of exquisite other-wordly beauty all around me. I felt like a Disney princess as I "tra-la-la-"d through the enchanting forest. The path itself was pretty well maintained and clear cut, but beyond the 30cm wide track grew dense trees, scrub and foliage like nothing I've ever seen in this country. To venture beyond the path would be to find oneself instantly lost with no way back. There were birds and squirrels everywhere. Noises of the jungle swirled around me in a cacophony of nature's music. I felt a thousand pairs of ambiguous eyes on me as I trudged through the sweltering heat. It was dark down here and I had hoped to be somewhat cooler from being out of the sun's blaze, but the forest canopy trapped in the heat like a sauna.

I was still trudging through a couple of hours later. I wasn't sure how deep into the jungle I was, or how much left of it there was still to hike through. When I looked back there was no light at the end of the tunnel, nor when I looked forward. I was growing tired, sweaty and running low on water. Feeling hot and bothered, a seed of panic started to rise in my stomach at being in here completely alone. I hadn't seen anyone else in here yet. There was no phone signal. It was just me. And my mind.

Until...

A pair of big deep brown eyes locked onto mine. I stopped dead in my tracks. My heart leapt into my throat, but then calmed just as instantly. The eyes belonged to the most beautiful deer I've ever seen sat nestled amongst the bushes about 10 feet away from me. She was fully grown with chestnut fur, a delicate face and pointed ears that pricked towards me. She stared straight into my core and spoke to me.
"Sit down, India. Pause. Stay a while. Be with me in this moment. Soak it all in." she said in the softest ethereal voice that reverberated around me like a harp.
"Ok. I will." I replied, taking my pack off and sitting down on the path directly opposite her.

I'm not sure how long The Deer and I sat looking at one another. But our eyes never left each other's. In the deep peaceful stillness of the wilderness we sat together. Fully present in the

beauty of our surroundings, connected to each
other on a soul level.

"Thank you." I said to her, a tear rolling down my
cheek.

She didn't reply with words. Just gazed at me
with those eyes that had seen a thousand
lifetimes. Known a thousand wisdoms. Told
infinite truths. Eyes with the depth and
expansiveness of the universe.

Eventually, after a few more miles wandering in
the jungle, feeling like I was floating on air after
my encounter with The Deer, I emerged out the
other side of the Undercliffs and onto the
outskirts of Lyme Regis. A couple approached
me, the woman in a floaty white sarong and
wide brimmed hat, the man in Hawaiian shorts
and flip-flops both carrying beach bags. They
looked like aliens to me after where I'd just been.

"Y'ahrite love, can we get t'beach down there?"
he said in a soft northern accent.

I looked at him in puzzlement as if he'd just
spoken a foreign language. It was a bit of a
culture shock to be around people again after
feeling like I'd spent an eternity in the Undercliffs
Wonderland. I'd almost forgotten how to speak.

"... we heard there's a beach off the path down
there is that right?" the woman ventured,
speaking slowly to me as if talking to a toddler.

"... Umm... Uh... oh, yes sorry. Haha, there's no
beach down there. There's no way you'll make it
through the Undercliffs wearing flip-flops either.
It's just five solid miles of thick jungle with only

one path through. I think someone was pulling your leg." I replied finally, finding my voice. The couple grumbled to each other a bit, feeling inconvenienced at the misinformation they'd received and I carried on my way not wanting to get caught in the crossfire.

Lyme Regis felt even more of a culture shock. The town was heaving with tourists and after popping into a supermarket to grab some food supplies, I quickly started walking out of the town and back onto my path.

I had hoped to climb the mammoth Golden Cap this afternoon, but the sun was so hot, it was over 30°C and I was tired after the 11 mile hike I'd just achieved. Golden Cap is the tallest peak on the south coast of Britain. I wanted to climb it with full energy, so I promised myself to wake up at the crack of dawn and do it first thing in the morning. And so, staggering into Charmouth, I went to Newlands campsite and bought my pitch for the evening. It was pricey, but I couldn't be bothered to barter for a discount with the receptionist and the luxurious showers made it so worth it.

After whizzing through my evening routine, eager to get a good night's rest, I collapsed in my tent, my eyes soon drooping after a wild, wonderful, amazing, life changing day. I will never forget that Deer for as long as I live, I thought to myself. The term "spirit animal" is thrown around a lot these days. Used almost in an ironic, comical way. But she really was. Deeply, profoundly, my spirit animal. I felt so grateful to have met her.

Day 51. I woke up slightly before 05:00am just as the milkiest hint of orange began to warm the night sky to the East. I flew through my morning routine and started walking on the coast path by 05:45am. I was determined. I will reach the top of Golden Cap in time for the sunrise, I promised myself. Starting the walking this early in the morning was so much easier. The sun had not yet risen, had not yet scorched the Earth with its ferocious heat and it made for much more comfortable hiking. I walked up and down lush farmland, the base of the mountain growing ever closer. I stopped for a nervous poo in a field full of cowpattes.

Then. There I was. There IT was. I stood at the bottom of Golden Cap at 07:15am with a steep 630ft climb to do. I chuckled to myself at the significance of the number 630. The sun was low in the morning dawn and had not yet risen over the peak and so it cast an atmospheric shadow over the land.
"Well. Here goes. Eek! Let's do it!" I motivated myself.

Breathe in. Breathe out. Breathe in. Breathe out. Push. One step in front of the other. Push. Arms swinging. Feet pounding. Heart racing.

Backpack creaking against my back. My eyes fixed to the path ahead. Push. I didn't stop. And then... at 07:30am... I planted my feet firmly on the peak of Golden Cap. It had taken me just 15 minutes to race up the shadowed side of the mountain.

"OH WOWWWWW!" I burst into tears. "OH WOW, OH WOW, OH MY GOSH, WOW!" were the only words that fell out of my overwhelmed brain as tears spilled from my eyes, hoarse gasps escaped my spasming throat and blood pulsated through the veins behind my ears. I'd just whizzed up Golden Cap in 15 minutes like a total boss babe but was totally stunned at the beauty around me.

The soft peach sun sat lower in the sky than I did, casting a gentle haze of honey glow over the landscape. The ocean was calm. The countryside was quiet. Life was still asleep. But I was here. Having just climbed the tallest peak on the south coast of Britain, crying my eyes out with joy, happiness, abundance and just pure awe at what I felt so thankful to be part of. I sat on the edge of Golden Cap for a long while. Dangling my legs into the vast space below. Probably not the safest thing to do, but I felt totally at ease taking a delicious moment to appreciate this reality.

This week was fast becoming my favourite week of hiking the SWCP. The weather was stunning, the scenery was breathtaking, my body felt so strong now and tackled the hiking with ease. I felt like I could continue walking forever. What a way to finish this life-changing journey.

I began the descent down to the holiday resort of Seatown where I popped into the shop there and treated myself to a cuppa and a cinnamon swirl as a way to congratulate myself. After that, mid morning, I reached West Bay and found myself feeling all nostalgic and emotional remembering many happy times as a child visiting my Grandparents who used to live here, strolling along the promenade hand in hand with them, eating vinegary fish & chips and 99 Flake ice creams. Before the constraints of religion got in the way.

There was a shop on the seafront called Aladdin's Cave that my brother and I loved to go to as kids. It lived up to its name - a stuffed haven of brick-a-brack, toys, buckets, spades, and tourist souvenirs that we could spend hours picking our way through. When I walked past it today though, I was sad to see it all boarded up and long shut down. The building carried an air of decay and loss.

The day was really hotting up now and I struggled getting up the next couple of cliffs past West Bay. Then passing Burton Bradstock, the path ran along a shingle beach for a few miles which was incredibly tough going. Every step, my boots sank into the shingle feeling like I was taking one step forward and two steps back. The heat rose off the beach in waves and my vision became blurry from the draining temperature. For mile after mile I trudged along, my boots seeming more leaden as the heat of the day rose and rose. I wondered when this terrain would ever end. I wondered will I ever find somewhere to camp tonight? Or will I be trying to sleep on hard pebbles out in the open under the stars? Am I about to collapse from exhaustion?

And then in the distance... laughter... music... a mirage? I came to a group of hippies in their late teens drinking Thatchers cider and smoking weed. Was this real? Had I passed out and this was some sort of hallucination? They sat around in a circle with a huge coolbox of ice in the centre filled to the brim with cool cider and other alcoholic beverages. They welcomed me with open arms and offered me cups of ice to drink and pour all over myself. I would've thought this was a dream had the shock of the ice cubes pouring on my burning skin not been enough to prove to me that yes, this was in fact real. I sat around with my lovely, kind new friends for a while, taking a breather, sharing my stories and cooling off, politely declining the offer of smoking a joint and drinking cider. They were such a lovely group of people and I felt proud that these would be the people of the future. This is the outlook on life, the love, the community that will heal humanity.

I said goodbye to my stoned saviours and eventually made it to West Bexington after a gruelling 15 mile, 10 hour hike. I reached the tiny car park there, finally stepping off the shingle terrain, my legs wobbled uncontrollably and then completely gave way beneath me. I collapsed in a heap, groaning.

"Fuuuuuuuuuuuuuuuck, that was haaaaaaard!!" I mumbled out loud, grimacing my eyes closed as sweat poured out of me.

"Oh my goodness are you ok? Here, have this water bottle, you need it!"

"Ugggggggghhh thank you so much!"

A kind couple just getting into their 4x4 gave me an ice cold bottle of berry flavoured water. I greedily drank it down as if it was the last water on Earth.

After sitting in the middle of the car park for a while, leaning against my backpack, legs stretched out in front of me, I decided that here is where I will find somewhere to camp tonight. I had hoped to make it a bit further to Abbotsbury but it's just too dangerously hot to go any further. The sun was scorching my skin even though I'd put a hundred layers of factor 50 sunscreen on.

I heaved myself up to standing. Feeling very wobbly now, my body begging me to stop for the day. I noticed some holiday chalets just behind the beach and stumbled up to them with the hopes that perhaps one of the occupants might let me stay in their garden for the night. And that's when my prayers were answered.

"Ooh my, are you ok there? You don't look too good?" said a petit middle aged lady with blonde-silver hair and a kind face.

"Not really, I'm hiking the SWCP for charity but I need to stop for the day, it's too hot! I wonder if I could ask a huge favour and perhaps camp in your garden tonight? It's just me and my tiny one man tent and I'll be gone as soon as the sun rises tomorrow morning!" I pleaded.

"Oh of course, love, you can stay in my garden no problem! My name's Judy. Come in and I'll get you a glass of water." she said.

"Oh thank you. Thank you so much, Judy, I'm so grateful. My name's India."

"Well very nice to meet you, India! And what an amazing thing you're doing! You deserve a swim in the sea once you're set up for sure."

"Thank you, great idea, I'll definitely do that."

Judy found a sheltered spot in the corner of her neatly maintained garden for me and I set up quickly, spending a few moments just resting in my tent in the late afternoon, drinking as much water as I could and feeling thankful that I'd found somewhere safe to sleep tonight. After a few moments rest, I dragged myself over to the ocean, stripped off to my undies and dived in the cool clear water. It was heaven. I brought my soap with me and washed the sweat and

sunscreen from my weather-beaten skin. I
allowed my tired body to just float in the salt
water. Bobbing up and down in the calmly
rippling ocran. It was so crystal clear I was almost
tempted to drink it... almost. The sun was now
hanging lower and lower to the West. At 6pm, I
got out of the water, patted my skin dry with my
microfibre towel and got dressed back into my
dirty, smelly clothes. I was used to that by now.

Back at my tent, I lay on top of my sleeping bag.
Still too hot to lie within it, I spent the evening
resting, massaging my body, reading my
guidebooks, the same beloved routine that felt
like second nature to me now. I looked into my
little pocket mirror and applied some of my foot
cream to my sun-kissed face. I gave a quiet gasp.
I couldn't remember the last time I'd properly
looked into a mirror. My face was a constellation
of freckles. My eyes were the brightest
green-grey-blue I'd ever seen them. My hair was
a wild, wavy, fiery mane of gold. I had blossomed.
All the epiphanies, all the realisations, all the
cultivation of self-love, all the challenges and
triumphs, were shining out of my face now in a
radiance I hadn't seen before.

Contentment lulled me to sleep before the sun
went down. My final thoughts of the day were a
swirling tapestry of memories made over the
past eight weeks. I was treasuring every last
moment on this path now.

Day 52. I woke up at 05:00am again to once again do the majority of the day's hiking in the cooler mornings. I thought it would be difficult to wake up so early, but in fact I was itching to get up and go. Because I'd discovered something truly awe inspiring. Hiking with the sunrise. I couldn't wait to see what today's offering would bring.

I discovered that Judy had left me a tea bag and some milk to make myself a cup of tea with in the shed in her garden and I wrote her a note to thank her for all the kindness she'd shown me. I raced through my morning routine, packed up all my things and started hiking at 05:30am. I walked three and a half miles along the South Dorset Ridgeway high up in the hills to Abbotsbury as the sun was rising and the views took my breath away. I cried tears of joy once again as the soft haze of dawn brushed over the vast expanse of Chesil Beach and the Isle of Portland in the distance. Rolling countryside blessed me with its presence everywhere I looked, with little settlements far in the distance dotted about here and there.

I got to Abbotsbury at 07:30am and dived into the corner shop there that had just opened for the day to restock breakfast supplies. I ran out yesterday, I only had four ration packs left which I needed to save for dinner times and hadn't had anything to eat yet this morning and so I was absolutely starving. The lovely owner restocked

my water from the tap in his kitchen as I
dithered in choosing the food I wanted. I wanted
it all. I bought a bag of granola, fresh fruit, a
couple of Cornish pasties, some bread and a
cinnamon swirl pastry. And my backpack felt all
the more heavy. But it was a sacrifice I happily
made. From there, it was a super pretty
cross-country walk through lush farmland down
to Abbotsbury Swannery, a nature reserve with a
big lake, home to a large flock of beautiful white
swans. It was so ridiculously beautiful all I could
do was just laugh out loud. Feeling infinitely
abundant and grateful at the beauty that exists
in this universe.

By 08:30am, it was getting extremely hot. Not a
cloud in sight. Just the fireball in the sky beating
down on the land. I was walking once again in
just my bra and leggings. And a hundred layers
of sunscreen that I was pedantically applying
every five minutes. From the Swannery, the path
wiggled its way down to the edge of the fleet of
water behind Chesil beach. This beach is a
fascinating natural structure. It's an 18 mile long
barrier of shingle with the ocean on one side and
a tidal fleet lagoon of water separating it from
the mainland. In places it is up to 50ft high and
650ft wide. Not really an island... but just a
gigantic wall of shingle beach protecting Dorset
from the waves of the English Channel. The
SWCP skirts the edge of the fleet on the
mainland. It is not recommended to walk along
Chesil Beach as it is extremely hard going and

there's no way to return to easier, more solid
ground on the mainland for 18 miles. I walked
the easy flat route along the fleet lagoon and
tried my best to stay cool. It was stiflingly hot
which made walking a lot harder than it
would've been normally. There wasn't much
opportunity for shade so every time I came
across a bush tall enough, I sheltered under it for
a few blissful moments.

At last, after a 12 mile hike, I made it to East Fleet
Campsite in the early afternoon where I planned
to stay for the next two nights because
tomorrow I will walk around the teardrop shaped
Isle of Portland. An official part of the SWCP that
is connected to the mainland via a two mile long
highway, and I thought I may as well stay in the
same place for the next two nights and enjoy
Portland tomorrow with just my day pack. I
strode into the campsite entrance and breathed
a huge sigh of relief as I stepped into the cool
air-conditioned reception area. Checking in with
the ladies at reception, they were intrigued
about what I was doing and I told them a brief
recap on my journey and why I was doing it.
"Ooh as you're doing it for charity, and it's just
you and your little tent, you can stay here for
free!" The lovely reception manager said.
"Oh my goodness, really? For both nights? I am
so grateful, truly, that's so kind of you, thank you
so much!" I said with a tear in my eye. Once
again, I was blown away by human generosity.

As I realised on the very first day of this walk, and the many days since: People Are Good.

I bought an ice cream and a cold drink from the little shop they have and skipped off to set up camp. I got a lovely shaded spot amongst a patch of soft grass and a lush tall green hedge behind me. And then I skipped off to the shower block.

Oh. My. Goodness.

These showers were the loveliest showers I've had so far. Each cubicle was like its own private bathroom complete with shower room, vanity area with a sink and a flushing toilet, all clad in lovely slate tile and dark wood. I felt like I'd stepped into a spa. And I was staying here for free! I couldn't help but pinch myself to check if this was really real. I stood underneath the water for a long time, soaking my dehydrated skin and hair with the life-giving tonic gushing from the waterfall showerhead.

After my shower, I floated back to my tent to enjoy the rest of the beautiful day relaxing, massaging my body, chilling out in the shade and just enjoying my own company. I reminisced a lot about how indescribably amazing these past eight weeks have been. Without doubt the best time of my life so far. I could feel that this was only just the beginning and there were so many more adventures to be had. But for now, I was cherishing every last precious second on this path. I had four more days left. I couldn't bear to think about what comes after yet. It was too painful to think about not being on this path everyday. I knew that a beautiful and wondrous life waited for me on the other side. But I just wanted to be here a little while longer.

"Let me stay in this cocoon a little while longer." I whispered out loud as the sun began to set on another magical day.

Day 53. Another stunning 5am start just before the sunrise this morning. I left my tent and belongings all set up at East Fleet Campsite ready for my return later this afternoon and packed my little daypack with all the food and water I would need. This morning, there was a delicious cool breeze that made walking all the more comfortable. I set off along the fleet lagoon's edge once more towards the start of the route around the Isle of Portland. It was much further away than I anticipated though. Two miles to the highway road, and then another two miles walking along the windy highway to reach the island itself. I calculated that that'll be eight miles of purely commuting to and from the island. And the route around Portland was 13 miles. I couldn't do 21 miles in one day in what was set to be another scorching day. So I decided that I would do a condensed version and see if I could find a smaller circular route around Portland.

I reached the Highway road and was greeted by a roaring stream of rush hour traffic travelling along the dusty road. There was a strong wind, but it was a choking hot wind fuelled with car pollution and sand from nearby Weymouth beach. But I powered walked along the flat highway anyway, getting into a good, fast, steady stride helped by having a much less heavy weight on my back.

Once I'd officially landed on the Isle of Portland, I chose a short five mile circular walk around the main town of Fortuneswell. I began the walk by treating myself to an amazing veggie breakfast fry-up at Quiddle's Café (the second breakfast after my own. Forever hungry as always.), a beautiful spot below the cliffs on the water's edge. After that, I began to walk up into the cliffs. The Isle of Portland is a peculiar place, I was quickly discovering. Its main attraction, if one could even call it that, is two large prisons, one an ex-navy base and one a young offenders institute, and it gives the island an air of bleakness. The landscape is very utilitarian. Lots of grey stone buildings covered in barbed wire, old dilapidated buildings and evidence of an old quarrying industry. It wasn't the most interesting place if I'm honest... but I felt satisfied that I'd got there all the same.

I walked to the top off the cliff to the Olympics monument and the views to the huge length of

Chesil Beach were stunning. Then I walked
down through Fortuneswell to Portland Castle,
then around the marina and then began the
long four mile walk back down the Highway and
along the fleet lagoon to East Fleet Campsite.
The wind was really picking up now on the
highway and I could feel my face becoming
filthy with pollution, dirt and sand. I could smell
a storm on the way... but no clouds around to
prove my senses.

On the long power walk down the highway, I
mused about what I'll do after my walk. What I
would do for work. For the past couple of years
I'd cultivated a little side hustle of making
handmade lingerie to empower women to fall in
love with their bodies. Even though I'd felt no
empowerment in myself until this year. Before
my walk, I thought I wanted to pursue that in
making it my full time business. But this walk
had changed everything for me. There was
something deeper there, something more I
wanted, no, NEEDED to share with women all
across the world to empower them to heal
themselves as I have healed myself. To save
themselves as I had saved my own life. What if
my lingerie business has just been the stepping
stone, the catalyst for that?

I'd been cooped up for so long. I want to taste,
feel, explore, experience all that this wonderful
Earth has to offer... I loved sewing but making
lingerie had become tiresome, too time

consuming and not financially viable for the time it took to make a set. How could I use my skills as a seamstress and love of dressmaking to empower women in other ways? I have many other passions in life too that I wanted to pursue. I wanted to share my story so that I can help heal humanity. I knew the answers would come in time.

Words were forming... paragraphs in my mind that I knew I had to write down and share with the world... a story of love, loss, heartbreak... and then of triumph, a reclamation... hiking, healing & a very long path...

I got back to my spot at East Fleet campsite, my mind buzzing with ideas. After taking a long soak in the shower, cooking dinner beside my little khaki tent, massaging my body, going through my evening routine like a practised meditation, I got out my journal, as I had done every night on this journey so I could record the day's events, and I began to write. I began to write this book. My hand struggled to keep up with my brain as thoughts poured from pen to paper. Scribblings, sentences, words that didn't yet have a structure but I knew would some day, hopefully, humbly, be a beacon of light to anyone needing guidance through a difficult time in their life.

As I began to drift off to sleep that evening, for the first time on this walk, I felt excited to finish. I had three days left. My heart and soul belonged on this path, to the wilderness of nature, and it always will. But now I was ready to go out into the world, to rise up out of my chrysalis and share all that I had learnt, all that Mother Earth had gifted me. I was ready.

Day 54. Another 05:00am wake up call again. My body clock was used to this easy pace of life now. I packed up all my gear and left the lovely East Fleet Campsite by 05:30am and decided that was easily my favourite campsite I'd stayed in so far, mainly because they were so lovely in letting me stay two nights for free. And the facilities were lush. I began the easy flat walk through the busy town of Weymouth, although at that time in the morning it was lovely and quiet, then along its long beachside promenade. After that, I stopped briefly at the tourist resort of Osmington Mills and got more food at the shop there. Then, ambling up into the hills, I walked past a very cool, funky festival-esque campsite called Eweleaze Farm and affirmed to myself that I must come back and stay a night in that place sometime in the future. It had many teepee tents, rainbow bunting everywhere, outdoor solar showers and just had a super cool vibe to it. The happy chilled out campers were all just waking up for the day and beginning their breakfast.

After that, it was a breathtaking walk up and down many white chalk cliffs and grassy valleys, every inch the picture postcard of the Jurassic Coast. There was a keen wind that refreshed my sun beaten skin. The landscape was so beautiful, looking like something from the Studio Ghibli film Spirited Away with the long grass rippling over the land mirroring the ocean waves. The colours of the landscape today had a certain brilliance and brightness that took my breath away. My eyes squinted at the sheer amount of light, but also wanted to be as wide open as possible to take in such beauty.

After an exhilarating 15 mile hike, I arrived at the famous Durdle Door. An iconic landmark rock formation, it's a natural limestone arch that protrudes from the land out into the ocean and looks like a portal to another world. The name Durdle comes from the old english "thyrel" meaning "hole". It's a tourist hotspot and today was no exception. People from all over the world were here to take pictures with this most peculiar alien-like structure.

I weaved my way through the crowd and up to the only campsite for miles around, the aptly named Durdle Door Campsite. Very generic and touristy but I wandered into reception anyway and asked if they had a little space for me to camp for one night.
"Of course! Welcome to Durdle Door! So for one person, one tent for one night, that's £37, please." said the smartly dressed receptionist in a black uniform.

"… Sorry, how much?!" I said my mouth agog, unsure whether I'd heard her correctly.

"… Yes, that's £37. That's our base camping rate per night." she replied, sheepishly.

THIRTY SEVEN POUNDS?! I screamed the figure in my mind. That is outrageously, ridiculously, criminally expensive!

"Seriously? But… but, it's just me! I'll hardly take up any space. All I need is a little corner and a tap for some water for one night. And…" I proceeded to briefly ramble my story to her, what I was doing and why.

"I'm really sorry, my hands are tied, we simply can't offer discounts. My boss, the campsite owner, he just wouldn't allow it. Believe me, I would let you stay for free if I could." she said.

I could tell she was being genuine. She really did seem tied up by the corporate powers that ran this place and I tried not to be angry with her.

"… Ok… I guess I'll just have to find somewhere else…" I said, trying my best to look forlorn, walking out the door in a last ditch attempt at even a sympathy discount.

But to no avail. I left the reception and wandered back out into the dusty campsite car park. The hot wind was really picking up now and my eyes filled with dry chalk. There were cars and people everywhere. Beeping at each other to get out of the way, jostling for space. There was a little shack with a lady selling coffee from it. I went up to her and asked her if there were any other campsites nearby.

"No sorry, love, this is your only option." she said with a kind face.

"I can't pay that amount of money, that's just daylight robbery! I guess I'll have to find somewhere to wild-camp..." I said.

"Oh, you can't do that either. The wardens will move you off pretty quickly. They do regular patrols of this entire area."

I walked away from the coffee shack. Aimlessly wandered around trying to find a sheltered spot that I could sneakily risk wild-camping in. But the landscape was very exposed. It was too windy to camp on the path right next to the cliff face. I had visions of my tent flying off the edge with me in it. I sat down, worn out after a long day, on a grassy patch outside the campsite entrance and pondered my options. I'd just enjoyed two nights for free at East Fleet. I only had two nights left on this wonderful journey. I didn't want to let anything spoil my last precious moments. These last two days, I wanted to wake up and feel as refreshed and comfortable as possible. So. I walked back into reception and paid the damn £37. They are certainly making the most of all the tourists that come here I thought.

The main camping ground was a very pretty wooded area. I quickly set up camp as a spot of rain arrived. I could hear thunder cracking in the distance as I wrote my journal in my tent. After that, I hop footed it to the shower block as the rain got heavier. Inside the shower block, I was bitterly disappointed. It was pretty scummy and the showers themselves were those god-awful push button ones that only give you five seconds of running water. Five seconds. Really. I counted it. I tried not to grumble too much about it though. I was safe and sound at least. Sheltered from the storm rumbling in. And cherishing every moment that I had left of this wonderful adventure. I fell asleep that night to the sound of heavy rain on my tent, thunder and lightning flashing right above me. But I felt warm and cosy. Two more days left. I've walked 600 miles in 8 weeks. There were just 30 left to do.

Day 55. My penultimate day. And my beloved path threw every challenge she could throw at me today as a parting gift. This morning I woke up early as usual, but on the tail end of the thunderstorm that had raged overnight. I'd quickly packed up all my wet things and got going, fully wrapped up in my waterproofs. I bid an eager farewell to Durdle Door campsite, vowing to never camp there again, and headed off to the stunning Lulworth Cove. By the time I got there, around 08:00am, I was completely soaked through. But there, just by the water's edge was an oasis in the form of a breakfast stall selling greasy fry-ups, builder's tea and sausage & bacon baps. The lovely lady running it greeted me warmly and I ordered a sausage bap with a fried egg and lots of ketchup. And a cup of tea of course. I sheltered from the rain under her canopy and greedily ate my breakfast as we chatted about our lives.

That breakfast was like rocket fuel to me. I felt strong and sustained for a big day of hiking. I left the breakfast stall and began walking around the shingle beach of Lulworth Cove. It is a stunning landscape here. You can see all the different types of rock and sediment that have built up over many millennia and it almost looks like a grey/brown/black rainbow. I began the steep climb up onto the cliff from the beach but the path had turned to a sludge of grey clay as dark and thick as the heavy clouds above me. My boots sank, slipped and slid all over the place and I laughed as my waterproofs got glazed head to toe in a slick of sludge.
"BRING IT ON, BABY! IS THAT IT?! GIVE IT TO ME!" I shouted into the heavy rain-filled sky. And I was really asking for the challenge. I asked my path to give it to me. Give me every experience today. Thrill me with every challenge, every struggle, every element of Mother Nature. I wanted to live and breathe it all.

At last I scrambled up onto the cliff tops, covered in wet clay and feeling like G.I Jane. which was appropriate as I entered the Lulworth Military Ranges. It's only open on weekends, and luckily today was a Saturday, so I skipped through the open gate and began the rollercoaster ride. And it really was a fascinating rollercoaster. Due to the rain, there was no one else about so it felt even more remote than I imagined. The path soared high up into cliff tops in the sky, then plummeted down into deep valleys. Around tiny coves and the odd eerie burnt out building. The rain continued to pour and I had to wring my shoes and socks out twice. On the second time, a young couple on a hike passed by me. Of course, being hikers, we stopped to chat for a while. Their names were Jonathen & Emily from London and they were hiking the SWCP for a week and staying in B&Bs along the way. Whilst we were chatting, the rain eased off and there was even a hint of sunshine on the horizon.

"Hey, why don't you sit down with us for a while and have a cup of tea?" Emily offered.

"Ah thank you so much I'd love that!" I replied.

And so I'd found yet more kindred spirits on this path and shared a few precious moments with these people who I felt so connected to, but I knew after this journey was over, I would never see them again. There was something beautiful, yet yearning, yet comforting about that and it got me thinking about all the other people I'd met over the past eight weeks. Fellow hikers on this path that felt like family. I wondered where their lives would take them next. I hoped it would lead them to something beautiful.

I said goodbye to Jonathen & Emily, continued on through The Ranges and emerged out the other side, eight miles later, at Kimmeridge Cove. The sun was well and truly out now and it was hot, hot, hot!

"Asked and you shall receive." my beloved path said to me as I tore off my waterproofs and began the next leg of the hike in my bra and leggings. I did indeed ask for every challenge she could throw at me. And I thrived on it. More steep valleys and high cliffs came, with more tricky clay terrain which was quite slippery at times. I pounded my feet against the ground, swung my arms by my side, grinned and cried and laughed and danced along the SWCP.

Until finally, I made it, 16 miles later, to Tom's Field campsite at Langton Matravers. I set up camp in the little Hiker's Field they had and settled in for my final evening. Every movement I made felt like a ceremony now. A sacred ritual.

I set up my little khaki green tent. Hammered in the tent pegs for the last time. Rolled out my thermal mat. Blew up my little blue travel pillow.

I took my last shower, savoured the running water cleaning my freckled, salted, clay embalmed skin.

I tore the second to last page out of my husk of a SWCP guidebook.

I wrote in my journal. Words that would one day soon form this very book.

I heated up my last military ration pack on my tiny camping stove. Bean stew. And savoured every bite of brown mush.

And throughout it all, I weeped. I embraced every emotion that came up. My heart and soul felt so filled with love that it overflowed from my eyes in salty tears, overflowed from my mouth in quiet sobs, overflowed from my body in gentle rhythmic swaying.

I was so incredibly happy. Yet sad. Excited. Yet grieving. Content. Yet hungry for what else this beautiful life had to offer.

The sun was setting behind some dramatic cloud formations way in the distance. And tomorrow... tomorrow... tomorrow.

Day 56. And just like that, my life-changing journey comes to an end. The finish line at South Haven Point was just 14 miles away. I took my sweet time today. There was no rush. I woke up early for the last morning routine. Got dressed into my cardboard-stiff clothes, I couldn't remember the last time I washed them. Ate my final oaty-nutty-protein-powdery breakfast concoction. Lovingly packed up all my things into my well-worn, well-loved backpack.

As I packed my toiletries away into my wash bag, I saw something squashed up at the bottom which intrigued me. It was a couple of sanitary pads and a couple of tampons and I realised I hadn't had a period for the past three months. Initial panic struck. But I hadn't had sex since the last time with my ex around eight months ago. "No, no way that's possible unless I'm the reincarnation of the Virgin Mary." I mumbled out loud to myself. I'd heard about women going on long thru-hikes before and losing their periods as a way of their bodies conserving energy and putting that energy into the actual hike and this reassured me somewhat. I trusted my body wholeheartedly and knew that, when she was ready, my cycle would return to normal. Which, sure enough, a month after I'd finished, it did.

I put my stinky boots on that now looked as grey and worn out as the first pair. Breathe. Take it all in. Let's do this.

I left Tom's Field campsite in the early hours of the morning and set off. The path felt easy-breezy today. A gentle ramble over low lying cliffs, past the beautiful Durston Castle, through the bustling town of Swanage, then up into the cliffs again onto the fascinating white chalk formations at Old Harry Rocks. I sat down and paused often along the way, this time not because I was tired, but because I really wanted to make sure to breathe in the exquisiteness of this earthly experience. This human experience. The weather was perfect. Cloudy but not raining. Not too hot, not too cold.

And then finally, I came to the beach at Studland Bay. I stood on the grassy verge at the edge of the sand. I'd just walked nonstop for 628 miles. There were just two miles left along this beach. It was busy. Families enjoying a day out. Kids splashing about in the water. Ice creams, windbreakers, sunglasses, paddleboards, buckets and spades. Emotion that I couldn't stop welled inside me and I began to cry. I could just turn around, I thought. I don't have to stop. I could just turn around and keep walking, I thought. And I seriously considered it for a moment. But alas. I couldn't.
"I have to finish this thing. It's time." I said out loud to myself.

I stepped onto the sand and walked. Sunday 25th of July 2021. Exactly eight weeks after I'd stepped onto the start line of the SWCP way back at Minehead. I was about to step over the finish line here at South Haven Point in Poole. Four counties, 630 miles, the equivalent elevation of climbing Mount Everest four times.

I sobbed loud gasps of raw emotion as my feet pounded the sand. Time seemed to stand still as people stopped what they were doing and watched me walk. And then, clapping. Was that the crashing waves I wondered? I looked at the ocean but it was calm. Where was that noise coming from? I looked inland. People were staring at me, standing up and clapping. I sobbed even more.

And then even more surreally, the final mile was a nudist beach. People wearing nothing but smiles on their faces clapped for me. I laughed and sobbed at the sight of them. Thanking them through my breathy gasps. You couldn't make this shit up, I thought to myself. An array of willies and breasts cheered me onto the finish line. I'd lost it. I'd completely and utterly lost it. Tears, snot, sweat, almost all the bodily fluids were gushing out of my face as I raced towards the end.

And then. Louder cheers. Whistles. Shouting. "INDY!!" "YOU MADE IT!" "WOOHOO GO INDY!" "COME ON DARLING YOU CAN DO IT!"

A quarter of a mile in the distance I saw the blue SWCP monument that marked the end of the 630 mile long trail. And gathered around it were my amazing family waving their arms in the air and cheering for me.

And there was nothing else to do. I ran to them. I ran like my life depended on it. My pack bounced up and down against my back, my feet sank into the sand, my legs and buttocks screamed at me to finally, properly rest. But I ran to my people. An endless stream of sobs poured out of my eyes and mouth.

And then, finally. At last. After 630 miles, 1014 kilometres, after 1,013,887 metres, millions and millions of steps, I collapsed against the blue SWCP monument in a heap of emotion. My family gathered around me in a flurry of excitement, giving me hugs, kisses, flowers, words of congratulations. I could barely take it all in, it all felt so surreal. So overwhelming. To have made it. I had just completed hiking the entire South West Coast Path. From beginning to end. It didn't feel real yet. On the road just behind the monument there was a traffic jam and the people in their cars had all turned their engines off, turned their music off, wound down their windows and watched me.

I took a moment. I lovingly asked my family to let me be on my own for a minute, as if I hadn't had enough of that already, but I needed a moment alone with my beloved path. It was all too much.

I wrapped my hands around the blue monument, closed my eyes and leant my forehead against its cool metallic surface. Breathed in the scent of the sea. Salty, sweet, with a hint of something sour. I embraced my beloved path.

"Thank you." I whispered to her, tears rolling down my dirty cheeks.
"Thank you. Thank you. Thank you. I love you."

There's that famous saying from J.R.R Tolkein, "Not all those who wander are lost." but there is another quote from Spanish poet Antonio

Machado that I resonate more with to my core. It is simply this:

"Wanderer, there is no path. The path is made by walking."

The day after The End.
But a New Beginning.
I've cried a lot today. Coming back to my flat after being gone for two months, unpacking my things and putting them away. Grief at what has come to an end. Happiness. Sadness. Pride at what I'd just achieved. Apprehension of what on Earth will I do now I don't have my path. Joy at the gloriousness of life itself. What a privilege it is to be alive. Oh, to feel the bittersweet pain in my heart at no longer waking up on the coast path. The yearning that stings my throat and prickles my eyes. But also the content feeling that I can always return to her whenever I need to. She will always be there. I will always be there. She will always be within me.

Everyday on the coast path I had been completely broken and then rebuilt like a piece of Kintsugi pottery. Every bone had been broken, then fused back together again, every muscle ripped apart, then stitched back together, every cell exploding, but rebirthing new stronger ones. With every cry, every meltdown, every tear that spilled down my dirty face, I was emerging, blossoming into the radiant woman that was always inside of me. The cracks in my heart have turned to gold.

I am both a new woman, and have rediscovered who I was deep down all along.
It's felt like coming home, but also surrendering to the unknown of the wilderness.
It's been heartbreaking and heartbuilding.
I've found myself whilst getting lost.
That's the only way I can describe this adventure: a beautiful paradox.
It's the wonder of the universe all rolled into one and it lives within me.

Epilogue

Two years later...

"Honey, look! Look at all that sea kale over there! Oh WOW!" she gasped with excitement. "Woah, I've never seen it grow so abundantly like that! Hey, let's pick some and cook it up on the campstove tonight." He replied with eager eyes.

It had been two years since the completion of her coast path saga, and now, she had returned, but with someone very special beside her. A kind, generous, honest man who had entered her life just two months after the 630 mile story ended.

They had come to hike the Jurassic Coast and she felt almost nervous as if she was introducing him to her parents for the first time. They'd packed up a couple of large backpacks, just like she had done alone years ago, with ration packs, a camp stove and a tent, and set off from West Bay for a three day hiking trip.

They were just approaching West Bexington, so many fond memories filling her mind. And now she was making new ones, with her love by her side.

They foraged a handful of crisp, juicy sea kale leaves and then took a long luxurious swim in the crystal clear ocean together. A welcome relief after the heat of the day.

She looked for the kind lady that had housed her in her garden two years ago, but sadly she was not home.

The couple walked up to Abbotsbury, marvelling at the stunning views of the South Dorset Ridgeway, and sneaked into an overgrown wildflower meadow to camp for the night.

"Ind, have you got those kale leaves?" He asked her lovingly as he cooked up a couple of vac-pac bean stew ration packs on the camp stove a little while later.
She smiled fondly and knowingly as she passed him the freshly chopped leaves. The sun was setting and washed the atmosphere in a cosy golden glow.

Dinner was absolutely delicious. They sat side by side on the grass in front of their little khaki backpackers tent and watched the sun set as they ate.

That night they made tender love under the stars. Skin to skin, a connection so deep, so profound, she was eternally grateful to experience it.

Her life had gone from strength to strength in the past two years. Meeting the man of her dreams, publishing the first edition of this very book, moving to Cornwall and forging a full time career from her seamstress work.

And none of it would've happened had it not been for the coast path. The call of the free, wild woman from deep within that she'd finally listened to had opened up her life beyond her imagination.

And all it took was to just go for a walk.

With Thanks

First and foremost I would like to thank my parents. You have been there throughout it all and continue to be there. You have been my safety net when I was free falling into chaos. You have been my biggest cheerleaders and taught me what unconditional love is. Thank you. B, J, M, you are the best little brothers a big sister could ask for. I love you crazy dudes.

To my darling Kev, you were literally by my side in our work studio as I wrote this book. Holding space for me as I relived all the emotions I had on this journey. In you I found a soul-partner. A love story more epic, more romantic than any novel I've read or movie I've seen. And thank you for creating the most beautiful book cover & map of the SWCP!

To Betsy. My sister. My best friend. My love. My chief manuscript reader. You are the yang to my yin. My constant. I am grateful for you more than you'll ever know.

Thank you to all the women in my life. You inspire me everyday. Bella, thank you for guiding me and holding me through my healing journey in those first tender months.

To Laura, thank you for the crystal clear advice in the muddy world of publishing books. This book may not have seen the light of day if it weren't for your generous and to the point emails!

Thank you to my SWCP family: Adam & Gemma, Phil & Lorraine, Catherine & Nigel, David, Daniel, Harry and the three lads Alastair, George & Aron. You provided companionship and encouragement during many tough days and just understood the journey. It was a privilege to walk with you. Also, many thanks to everyone I met on the trail for all your words of encouragement and endless cups of tea!

And to you dear reader, thank you for sticking with me along this epic tale. If you picked this book up, chances are you're working through something in your life. I see you. I hear you. I feel you. And to you I say: go for a walk. Put one step in front of the other and the answers you seek will come. This book is dedicated to you.

And last, but certainly not least, thank you to my beloved path. The South West Coast Path. Who I continue to come back to again and again. Many of life's worries, big decisions and celebrations have been witnessed by you. You have washed away my tears, provided solid ground for my restless footsteps to pound against, blown out the cobwebs in my mind, nourished me, healed me, fulfilled me time and time again. Thank you. I love you.

Photo taken by Aron Hosie @aronhosie

Photo taken by India Hicks

Photo taken by India's Mum

Campsite Directory

Here you'll find the list of campsites that I stayed at and recommend if you wish to embark on your own adventure and need some places to stay. All information correct at the time of writing, January 2024.

North Devon
- Newberry Campsite, Coombe Martin, North Devon , EX34 0AT www.newberryvalleypark.co.uk 01271 882334
- North Morte Farm Campsite, Woolacombe EX34 7EG, www.northmortefarm.co.uk 01271 870381

Cornwall (North Coast)
- Upper Lynstone Campsite, Bude, EX23 0LP, www.upperlynstone.co.uk 01288 352017
- Southwinds Campsite, Polzeath, PL27 6QU, www.polzeathcamping.co.uk 01208 863267
- Dennis Cove Campsite, Padstow, PL28 8DR, www.denniscovecampsite.co.uk 01841 532349
- Carnevas Campsite, Porthcothan, PL28 8PN, 01841 520230
- Quarryfields Campsite, Newquay, TR8 5RJ, www.quarryfield.co.uk 01673 830338

- Perranporth Campsite, Perranporth, TR6 0DB, www.perranporth-camping.co.uk 01872 572174
- Mount Pleasant Eco Park, Porthtowan, TR4 8HL www.mpecopark.co.uk 01209 891 500
- Gwithian Farm Campsite, Gwithian, TR27 5BX, www.gwithianfarm.co.uk 01736 753127
- Trevaylor Campsite, Botallack, TR19 7PU www.cornishcamping.co.uk 01736 787016
- Land's End Camping, Trevescan, TR19 7AQ, www.landsendcamp.co.uk 07376 535822

Cornwall (South Coast)

- Treen Farm Campsite, Treen, TR19 6LF, www.treenfarmcampsite.com 07598 469322
- Mousehole Camping, Mousehole AFC, TR19 6AZ, www.mouseholecamping.co.uk 07470 920006
- Higher Pentreath Farm Campsite, Praa Sands, TR20 9TL, www.higherpentreathcampsite.co.uk 01736 763240
- Henry's Campsite, Lizard, TR12 7NX, www.henryscampsite.co.uk   01326 290596
- Little Trevothan Campsite, Coverack, TR12 6SD, www.littletrevothan.co.uk 01326 280260

- Treloan Coastal Holidays, Portscatho, TR2 5EF, www.treloancoastalholidays.co.uk 01872 580989
- Treveor Farm Campsite, Gorran Haven, PL26 6LW, www.treveorfarm.com 01726 842387
- Penhale Farm Campsite, Par, PL23 1JU, www.penhale-fowey.co.uk 01726 833425
- Great Kellow Farm Campsite, Polperro, PL13 2QL, www.greatkellowfarm.co.uk 01503 272387
- Bay View Campsite, Looe, PL13 1NZ www.looebaycaravans.co.uk 01503 265922

South Devon

- Mount Folly Farm, Bigbury, TQ7 4AP www.bigburyholidays.co.uk 01548 810079
- Seaview Campsite, Slapton, TQ7 2RB www.camping-devon.com 01548 580366
- Salcombe Regis Campsite, Sidmouth, EX10 0JH, www.salcombe-regis.co.uk 01395 514303
- Axmouth Campsite, Seaton, EX12 4AF, 01297 24707

Dorset

- Newlands Holiday Park, Charmouth, DT6 6RB, www.newlandsholidays.co.uk 01297 560259
- East Fleet Farm Campsite, Weymouth, DT3 4DW, 0330 053 700

- Tom's Field Campsite, Langton Matravers, BH19 3HN, www.tomsfieldcamping.co.uk 01929 427110

Thank you again to all the kind souls who run these sites for your words of encouragement, cups of tea and generous help on my journey!

Printed in Great Britain
by Amazon

43903449R00142